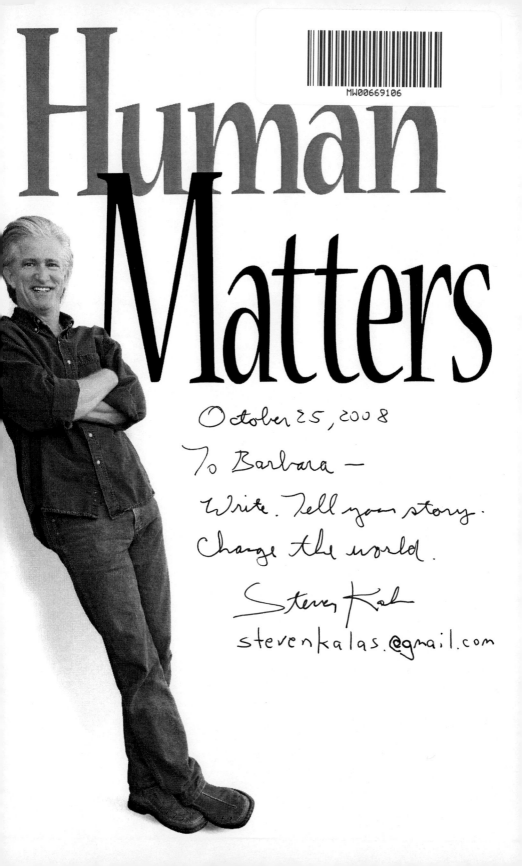

Human Matters

October 25, 2008

To Barbara —

Write. Tell your story.
Change the world.

Steven Kalas

stevenkalas.@gmail.com

Human Matters

Wise and witty counsel on relationships,
parenting, grief, and doing the right thing

Steven Kalas

Stephens Press · Las Vegas, Nevada

Editor: Geoff Schumacher
Book Designer: Sue Campbell
Author photographer: Dale Dombrowski
Publishing Coordinator: Stacey Fott

Cataloging-in-Publication

Kalas, Steven.
   Human matters : wise and witty counsel on relationships, parent-ing, grief and doing the right thing / Steven Kalas ; introduction by Sue Chance.
   216 p. ; 23 cm.
Contents: Children, parents, and family matters – Male and female mat-ters – Grief and loss matters – Values matters – Authenticity matters – Spiritual matters – Observing matters – Recommended reading.
ISBN-10: 1-932173-57-9
ISBN-13: 978-1-932173-57-4
1. Grief. 2. Interpersonal relations. 3. Parenting. 4. Psychology, Applied. I. Title.

158.2--dc22   2008   2007938113

 STEPHENS PRESS, LLC
A Stephens Media Company

Post Office Box 1600
Las Vegas, NV 89125-1600
www.stephenspress.com

Printed in United States of America

To Ruth Tiffany Barnhouse, 1923–1999,
my mentor and my friend.

CONTENTS

Wit, Wisdom, and Human Matters

What do you want when you read a columnist whose specialty is human matters? The first thing most of us want is intelligence, and you definitely have it here. Probably the first runner-up on our wish list is someone who can render sophisticated concepts in plain terms. Anybody who has spent much time in classrooms knows the value of this. It's how we define "good teachers," and we suspect, correctly, that the person who explains things the clearest understands them the best. Those who rely on jargon and specialized language have a very different goal, such as making themselves look good or obscuring something they'd rather you didn't know about. Think governmental body of your choice here.

Let me give you an example of that clarity, taken from Steven Kalas' writing. On the ever-touchy subject of religion, he says, "Few things are more potentially lethal than people who cannot psychologically distinguish between God and their own infantile ego needs. More simply, bad religion exacerbates the already breathtaking human propensity for hatred and violence." Watch the news if you don't understand that one. It'll come to you.

There are also shocking but illuminating statements such as, "I'm no respecter of the runaway train of collective narcissism that is this culture." Now there's a whole entire subject in a nutshell.

Next, I think most of us appreciate a columnist who is a little unorthodox. Not that he is disrespectful of our ways of thinking and being, but that he will sometimes turn things upside down and make us see them in a new way. That happy circumstance will make us say, "I never would've thought of that/seen it that way/explained it like that," and we're usually very pleased because we sense something has been added to our lives.

Another way of saying that is we want a writer with the ability to surprise, and with that, delight us. I remember coming to the end of *Charlotte's Web*, and laughing with tears in my eyes as I read, "Wilbur never forgot Charlotte. . . . It is not often that someone comes along who is a true friend and a good writer. Charlotte was both."

There's a feeling of that same friendship with a good writer here. Our media-saturated world seems to create a thirst for an honest-to-God dialogue with someone who loves to talk. Not at you, but with you. Read Steven and you feel included. It doesn't matter that the two of you aren't speaking out loud; you're conversing in your minds, and that's no small thing. He sees you the way Charlotte saw Wilbur — not as the runt of the litter, destined to become pork roast and bacon, but as "Some Pig!" There's a sense of wonder when he looks at people, recognizing the things we hold in common, but celebrating the differences. The acknowledgement that you are struggling with many of the same things he is comes attached to credit for your efforts. Only a person with well-developed empathy and compassion for others sees the world that way. Only those with a rock-solid sense of fair play understand the necessity of telling people what's right with them. After all, there are plenty of "helpful" gurus, family, and friends who'll tell you what's wrong with you.

One tremendous bonus is that he demystifies therapy. For example, he speaks of a woman determined not to cry, even though whatever she's brought to the table hurts like stink. Instead of giving her "permission" to cry, he helps her see that she's making up the rule that says to cry is wimpy, an imposition on the other, negative behavior, poor communication skills, etc. He gives you a glimpse of that holy containment field, that loving, respectful space where people perform the Herculean task of changing their minds and behavior to something more humane to themselves and others. Or, to say it in his classic way: "Therapy isn't about what I want to know about you. It's about what you'd like to know about you."

If you're an avid reader, you know that books can take us places where we wouldn't otherwise go. He shares his love for and admiration of Atticus Finch, and since you share that love for an ideal father and a man for whom self-respect was everything, you totally get what he's saying about fatherhood. When he invites you into the therapeutic relationship, he's showing you a paradigm for relating that's transferable to all aspects of your life. Shut up and honestly listen to others. Say what you mean and mean what you say. Well, yeah. That's a down and dirty definition of integrity, and Atticus has it in spades. So does Steven.

It also takes a special kind of fearlessness to bring up the things that trouble us and make us blush, admitting that we've made complete fools of ourselves over those things innumerable times. But so what? Good columns or essays aren't about wallowing in our mistakes; it's about admitting them, then appreciating what we've learned from them. He does that over and over, sometimes with honesty that burns through to the bone and sometimes with a wink and an aside that makes us laugh out loud. My personal favorite is when he is asked if he's ever had the urge to wallop one of his kids. He says, "Oooh, baby."

There's a serious discussion about the death penalty, focusing on Timothy McVeigh, that ends, "How surprising are the mysterious layers and contradictions of the human experience! If you ask my head, I'll tell you that the death penalty is immoral and unhelpful. I'm against it. If you ask my heart, at least as it regards certain capital crimes, it turns out I can wish you dead." Remember what I said about burning to the bone?

On the other hand, there's a discussion of the crazy-making inconsistencies of airport security, then his: "Some days, as I slog through airport security, not sure whether to laugh maniacally or bleat, not sure if I'm watching security check or watching a sale at Payless Shoes . . . some days I give serious thought to putting all my clothes in the gray plastic tub and walking through the metal detector with nothing but a smile."

See, I believe that poking a bit of fun at ourselves is the best possible evidence that we're integrated. He says this elegantly when he writes, "As human beings, we have integrity when the myriad aspects and attributes of our humanity are properly related within ourselves. When we are properly related, we find inner strength, and authentic action proceeds." One of those authentic actions is acknowledging how utterly silly we are at times and yet acknowledging our own good-heartedness. We give ourselves credit at the same time we take a pratfall. For instance, he writes, "When I bump into someone on Aisle 4 at the grocery, I say 'excuse me,' which is shorthand for 'I confess that, in my quest for Polish Dill Spears, I constructed my own special universe and lived for a moment as if I was the only person whose existence mattered. Turns out you and your grocery cart live in my universe, too. My bad.'"

Gee, don't you wish some of the people who ram you while talking on their cell phones would develop this level of insight? The world would definitely be a better place.

I'm going to let him explain his concept of radical responsibility, because excerpting would be detrimental in that case, but I cherish these lines: "Wish I had a nickel for every celebrity I've ever seen on a talk show who smiles a superior, enlightened smile, nods like the Buddha, and says meaningfully, 'I have no regrets.'

"May I be frank? If you have no regrets, then take a hike. I don't want to know you. Because, while you might have been a 'being,' you've never been a human being. Human beings have regrets. Buckets of them."

Feel free to stand up and cheer at this point.

I'm convinced there's no subject Steven won't tackle. And Holy Cow, does that mean taking on holy cows! While he's doing it, there is a golden vein of what it means to be fully human and he mines that with great capability and wit.

In this book, there are asides that will catch you off guard in the best possible way. Here and there, you'll notice the deft flick of a metaphor that'll illuminate something that's puzzled and eluded you. You'll notice his special access to himself, especially his child self, and you'll see it in both its painful honesty and its joy-inspiring playfulness. You'll find wisdom, for all that that particular word makes many of us cringe. You might slap your forehead at some point and say, "It's the honesty, stupid." You'll laugh when you come across pithy comments like this: "It's better to give than to receive. It's also a whole lot easier."

If you're looking for a columnist/writer who can deliver all the above, Steven Kalas is your man.

—**SUE CHANCE, M.D.**

Sue Chance, M.D., is a retired Menninger-trained psychiatrist and a former columnist living in South Carolina.

The upside of being born compulsively verbal is that you can talk your way into and through almost anything. You can be interesting. Entertaining. You can make people laugh. You can put people at ease. You can compel and charm your elementary school teachers; you can compel and distract your secondary school teachers. You can become a public speaker, and in so doing render benign the number one social phobia — the fear of public speaking.

The downside of being compulsively verbal is that you can become lazy. Words can hide as much as they reveal, muddy as much as they clarify. The ability to think deeply, clearly, critically, and to know oneself requires silence and contemplation. Too much work. The temptation is to chatter on.

Excellence in the spoken word requires an above-average verbal I.Q., a reckless self-esteem, and some experience. Excellence in the written word requires a much greater intention. The written word is deliberate. The written word has a delete key. A word once spoken can be explained, denied, illuminated, obfuscated — but never deleted.

I'm convinced the written word is eminently more powerful.

I somehow got all the way into my third semester of graduate school without ever learning to write. Then I met the Rev. Ruth Tiffany Barnhouse, M.D., Ph.D.

Dr. Barnhouse had come to my graduate school with great aplomb. She was an Episcopal priest, a Jungian analyst, a psychiatrist, author, international public speaker — an academic juggernaut. She was a brassy, sassy New Englander. She smoked. Mean smart. The mother of seven children. She laughed a lot, and her cackle would pour out of her office and float all the way down the hall.

In my third semester, I took my first class from Dr. Barnhouse. In the second week, she assigned us the task of reading an article and writing a 1,000-word response. I went back to my dorm room. I read the article. I wrote my response. I turned it in right on time.

A few days later, I found my paper in my mailbox at the student center. My paper was an ocean of red ink. Looked like a piece of evidence from an Alfred Hitchcock movie. And, at the bottom of the page, where there should have been a grade, there was instead printed in small block letters:

"THIS PAPER IS SO POORLY WRITTEN, I HAVE TROUBLE JUDGING ITS CONTENTS."

Ouch.

I was furious. I stormed to her office and knocked on the door. "Come in," she said, her voice bouncing off her palate and up through her nose in that dry New England drawl.

I let her have it. Spewed my indignation. On and on. Nobody had ever talked to me that way.

And through it all she sat behind her desk and stared, frozen, cigarette ignored in her left hand. When I was done, she raised her brow, pursed her lips, shrugged her shoulders palms up, and said: "My mistake. I thought you'd chosen a career path as a professional communicator."

Not even my ego was big enough to fake an intelligent response.

I can't say, really, that Dr. Barnhouse taught me to write. She more referred me to a couple of books and insisted that I get off my duff and learn to write. Right now.

See, I'm not much of a self-starter. The fastest way to get excellence out of me is to provide me leaders for whom my respect is so great I could never bear their disappointment.

A year later, during yet another clinical debate (which I'm sure I was losing), she surprised me by saying, "Call me Ruth." She liked me. Admired me. And no human being is more responsible for my intellectual, academic, and professional development. I took every class she offered. Read everything she wrote. We never lost touch.

Nineteen years later: She called me two days before she underwent surgical repair on an aortic aneurism. She said she was nervous, given that she, at seventy-six, "was no spring chicken (cackle, cackle)." I reassured her. Prayed with her. Told her I loved her.

Ruth never really came out of that surgery. Old Blue Eyes died on May 18, 1999. Thinking about her always begins a dance of breathtaking emptiness, overwhelming gratitude, and a huge lump of vulnerability in my throat.

I like the dance.

Writing a column like Human Matters twice weekly for the *Las Vegas Review-Journal* is a bit like sitting on the wrong side of a one-way mirror. The vulnerable side. The side where people can see you, but all you see is your own reflection.

I meet readers all the time who respond to me like I was their first cousin, or kid brother, or old college roommate. They know things about my children. They know some stories of my personal successes and equally personal failures. They know a few things — thank God only a few things — about my love life. My spiritual life. My passions and my politics. They know something of my character, and its absence. They have a sense of my honor, my values, and my darkness.

You see, it all leaks out eventually. What I don't say, you can infer. Some people thank me for "being so courageous" as to share myself so personally. Other people pretty much think I'm an exhibitionist.

They're both right. Creative writing is art. And art, if it is art, always includes the autobiography of the artist. Subtly or not so subtly. But always.

I write for the same reason other people ride roller coasters. It puts endorphins in my brain stem. Exhilarates. I'm responsible for these words, yes, but not altogether in control. I can't anticipate the turns up ahead.

Like most writers, I sit and fidget. Stare at the screen. I play computer solitaire. Check my e-mail. It seems I have to learn again each time that thinking about writing isn't writing. Wishing to write isn't writing. Chafing under a deadline isn't writing. Thinking profound thoughts isn't writing. Having a great idea in the shower isn't writing.

Only writing is writing. The only way to access that mystical flow is to start pressing the keys and see what happens.

I write for the same reason that little kids play with Legos. Just as it's always the same Legos in the bag, well, it's always the same words in the dictionary. The fun is finding new ways to put them together. I like giving readers pause. I like snapping their heads around and making them say, "Whhaaat?" I like inviting readers out on to a branch, sneaking behind them and sawing it off. I like making people laugh, only to realize too late that they are laughing at the truth. They are laughing at themselves.

I like irony. I think Julian satire is simply delicious. I like *italics*. Sentence fragments.

Human Matters comes from a place inside my awareness that is like carrying a camera, always ready to take snapshots of life. Could be a snapshot of something in the news, something on television, something on a bumper sticker or billboard. A two-sentence exchange between a convenience store clerk and patron. Lovers holding hands in a parking lot. A mother and her toddler in the grocery store.

Then I enlarge the shot. Look at it. Examine it. Talk about it. Learn from it.

More than anything, I like pushing myself to think. I like making the reader think. I like to make it more difficult to think in old and familiar ways. Agree or disagree, but there is no higher compliment for me than "You made me think," or "I'll never think about that the same way again."

Without you, the reader, it would be forever a monologue stuck inside my head. But when you read *Human Matters*, when you're willing to think with me and maybe even to write to me, it becomes a dialogue. And I think dialogue rocks.

Thanks for reading, and for taking the time to write.

Children, Parents, and Family Matters

I'M A DINOSAUR OF SORTS, I GUESS, BECAUSE I STILL BELIEVE DEEPLY THAT THE FAMILY IS THE BEDROCK OF THE DEVELOPMENT OF HUMAN BEINGS. Yet I'm stunned by the way modern family ideology and practice have desperately isolated individual families from the wider resources found in healthy community.

I once watched a presidential nominee make a fist and say out loud, with just the right combination of indignation, passion and scolding, "It doesn't take a village to raise a child! It takes a family!"

You would think it was the Second Coming. You would think Paris Hilton just successfully filled out a job application at Wal-Mart. Hosanna heysanna ho. The audience gave the nominee a two-minute standing ovation.

The nominee was referring, of course, to the now-famous African parable: It takes a village to raise a child. The nominee disagreed, and his fans were relieved and delighted that someone finally had the courage to put this misguided, cross-continental colloquialism in its place.

"Wow," I think. It doesn't take a village. It takes a family. I wonder where your family lives, Mr. Nominee.

Mine lives in a village.

My first son was given a score of "10" on the measure of an infant's predictability to thrive. Utterly healthy. He was born to two parents, each married to the other, each with a job, neither with addictions or criminal records. Between his mom and I were three college degrees. More or less competent adults.

And in about thirty-six hours it was obvious to me that one healthy baby required more than two competent people could provide.

Thank goodness we had access to a healthy village. Grandparents, aunts, uncles, adult cousins, close friends, folks from church — people rotated through our home in those first crucial weeks helping, holding, bathing, feeding, cooking, grocery shopping. Later our village included neighbors, day-care providers, librarians, teachers, police officers, physicians, and even George Carlin and Ringo Starr (the erstwhile conductors on the children's TV show *Thomas the Tank Engine*).

Today I have three children. I'm a single parent. A healthy village is more crucial to me than ever before.

Modern politics would have us choose between the idea of family and the idea of a village. But that's ridiculous. I'm all for family. And . . . your family lives in a village whether you wish it did or not. The village is going to profoundly influence your family, whether you wish it did nor not. Beyond that, the finest dad and the finest mom in the world cannot — I repeat, cannot — give a child everything needed for a full and happy life. Sooner or later, you'll find yourself needing to rely on the village.

Part of any parent's job is to pretty much always be soliciting, nurturing, and expanding the village relationships. And not just for child-rearing — extended family systems nestled dynamically in healthy villages are a great place to be an adult who sometimes needs a hand up, who someday grows old, weak, and vulnerable.

This culture's prejudice for the nuclear family is just that. A prejudice. One mom. One dad. Some kids and maybe a dog. Everybody else butts out. Folks, virtually no other civilization, past or present, raises children with that mind-set.

Nuclear family is an apt moniker, though. It's the family most likely to blow up in a mushroom cloud.

We see ourselves in our children, for better or for worse

My then two-year-old first born had discovered the playground slide at church. I lifted him to the top, placed my hands maybe eight inches in front of him, and he leaned forward into my embrace. I would then slide him down at about one-third the speed that gravity would have otherwise done.

"Wheeee," I said.

"Wheeee," he echoed.

And then at the bottom: "Doot again."

Eighty-seven times he said, "Doot again." Days of wonder.

One week later. "The Whee," my boy pointed and exclaimed. I placed him on top of the slide. He looked down. He balked. "No, Papa, down."

What happened next all occurred in about seven seconds, but it takes longer than that to describe.

I was angry. It started in my chest, bloomed into my throat, and banged against the back of my face like the heat bloom of a nuclear reactor. I felt contempt for the boy's anger, but it was also a personal slight, as if to say, "How dare you even consider the possibility that I might let you fall?"

And, for the first time in our relationship, I hesitated. I withheld empathy. The boy reached for me, and I did not immediately reach to comfort him.

What saved me — saved us, actually — was a spontaneous memory. It's 1963, and I'm standing in the midway of the Arizona State Fair. I'm staring up at my father, crying. (I think with a part of myself I shall always remember my father from the vantage point of a thirty-eight-inch six-year-old.) My father is heaping contempt on me because I'm afraid of the rotating tunnel at the end of the Funhouse. Instead of braving the tunnel, I walked around it past a large sign of a chicken.

Fear was against the rules at our house, and I was afraid a lot as a child — afraid of going too fast, afraid of climbing too high, afraid of falling down. Mostly I was afraid of my father. And I hated myself for being afraid.

It hits me like a lightning bolt: I don't despise my son for his fear; I despise myself. My son isn't doing anything wrong. He's just being two. But in this moment, he's like "mirror, mirror, on my son. . . ." His spontaneous, uncensored self is making me look at me. And I hate the part of me that feels afraid. It feels like I have contempt for my son. The real contempt is for myself.

In one quick movement I lift the boy down from the slide, hand him to his mother, and walk away muttering to myself:

It's okay if he's afraid of the slide. There's nothing at stake for you or for him if he spends the rest of his life afraid of slides. If he's thirty-seven and still afraid of slides, IT'S FINE. It's no reflection on you or his manhood. Everything will be okay.

Then my reflection moves deeper. I'm sad and grateful at the same time. Sad, because self-loathing is a lonely business. I'm sad about the way I was treated. Grateful, because, when you don't have the father you wanted, it's a wonderful compensation to try to be the father you most wanted to have.

One of the greatest gifts we can give our children is to take seriously our history with our own caregivers — what they were and what they were not. When we find the gumption to see our parents as they really were and are, we are freer to celebrate their gifts to us . . . and to hand back the unwanted baggage. When we find the candor and courage to live consciously with issues of injustice, cruelty, and abuse, we discover that we are much less likely to re-enact those same sins with our children.

Or, as I often say, my goal is not to be a perfect parent. It's just that I'd like to make new mistakes. Preferably ones that don't involve hitting, contempt, or humiliation.

Adults need to remember the joy of having fun

My son asks to go to Sky Mania for his fourteenth birthday. Sky Mania is a great big metal barn housing an acre of trampolines. Trust me when I say you have never seen so many trampolines in one place. The trampolines are bordered . . . by trampolines. Yes. You can even hurl yourself against the side of the room. At Sky Mania, kids are literally bouncing off the walls.

So my boy sorts out his guest list and here we are, two adults and four eighth-graders wearing these little wristbands saying we can jump from six o'clock to seven.

With a few minutes to kill, I go next door. Indoor skateboarding and biking. You know, the daredevils who swoop up and down those huge horseshoe inclines, twisting supernaturally in the air. How does the skateboard stay stuck to the kid? Velcro? These kids are good. Exciting to watch.

Back to Sky Mania. We gather for orientation. No sitting on top of the walls. No double flips. It's against the rules to sit or lie down on the trampolines. If we need to rest, we have to come back here. How silly, I think. I paid to jump. Not to rest.

Twenty-five minutes later I'm lying on the sideline. Not sure how I made it back. I'm drenched with sweat. Breath coming in heaves. "Is your dad okay?" I hear my son's classmate ask. Nothing wrong with me that quality hospice care couldn't fix, I think. Words like meniscus, patella, and lateral co-lateral ligament come to mind.

But as it looks like I might live after all, I sit and watch. It looks like a Spider-Man convention. Or a meeting of the Secret Society of Frog People. Or a bunch of ping-pong balls. These kids aren't merely having fun; their very bodies are rejoicing. I don't see auras, but it's easy to imagine green-white light exploding from the solar plexus every time they rocket their bodies into the sky. They whoop. They laugh. They scream "whoa" a lot. Paroxysms of joy.

These kids aren't burning down any gymnasiums. There are no bullies here. These are not fat kids downing Cheetos while their eyes glaze over watching Sponge Bob. No one is dealing drugs or using tobacco, except a few death-wish adults on the suicide installment plan.

In this room, the kids are fearless. They aren't even afraid of fear. Which means they feel safe.

Ironic, because kids do get hurt. There's a young girl with an ice pack on a twisted ankle. Two boys bang heads, and a few tears spill. I think this is a place where bruises and bumps happen as a matter of course. Maybe even an occasional chipped tooth.

Come to think of it, how does this place stay open? Or the skaters' paradise next door? I might be looking at the last place in America where kids are having fun on their own terms. As opposed to "fun" assigned to them by grown-ups, progressive educational philosophies, and insurance liability actuarial tables.

At Sky Mania, the adult staffers are present, alert, and provide all the necessary supervision. But they don't intrude. Most of them are just big kids themselves.

Fun for its own sake? It's a lost art in America, especially for adults.

When I was a boy, I would go to my friend's house, knock on the door, and ask my friend's mom the $64 Million Question: "Can Paul come out and play?"

I mean, think about the question. For kids, fun is a very intentional and specific agenda. You ask for it out loud. If and when adults play at all, they have to pose the question indirectly: Wanna stop by for coffee? Wanna meet for lunch? Adults stash their fun in the ceremonial accident of eating, drinking, or sensible activity.

Or they say, "Hey, Steven, would you like to spend several hours dropping $200 in a video poker machine while breathing second-hand smoke and listening to DING-DING-DING-DING and drinking unlimited free Coronas served by a woman who SO should not be wearing that outfit? After that we could go to a nightclub and shout at each other and breathe more smoke and drink more."

Casinos and nightclubs exhaust me. Sky Mania exhausts me. But the two states of exhaustion are somehow very different. I'm convinced human beings should play more. Fun is underrated.

Societal fears rob kids of male mentors

I met Rex one Sunday morning in 1968 when my family was out "church shopping." I was in the sixth grade. Today, Rex is a retired Methodist minister enjoying life with his wife, Margaret, his daughter, his grandson and his many passions and hobbies. My youngest son, Joseph Rex, is named after him.

Rex is the closest thing to a father I will ever have.

I wasn't dealt a very good hand when it came to fathers. I didn't meet my birth father until I was eighteen years old. Another man married my mom and then adopted me when I was three. It is his name I bear. Today, he and I bear together the estrangement born of disrespect, too-frequent humiliation, occasional violence, and, most importantly, the singular absence of accountability for the troubled history between us.

And so, at age eleven, I met Rex. I was drawn to him like the face of a flower to the sun and rain. I didn't know it at the time, but he was drawn to me, too. I hung around his office on Sunday mornings. He gave really good hugs, always genuinely glad to see me. He openly and warmly admired me. I clung to him at every chance, drawing from his energy some divine recompense for the fears and wounds that absent fathers and anti-fathers had brought me.

Later, when I acquired a driver's license, I was a frequent visitor to Rex's house. I shadowed him as he worked silver and turquoise in his lapidary. He showed me his guns and told me stories of hunting. I helped him with yard work.

We'd sit for hours around his backyard fire pit in the winter and talk about my struggles at home, about God, girls, career, school, romance, heartbreaks, sports, and sex. (Okay, for a couple of years there, during my adolescence, we talked a lot about sex.) We went to Phoenix Suns basketball games. We went to movies. We went camping. All in all, it's likely Rex saved my life.

And the story you've just read might never happen again.

If I was an eleven-year-old today, bearing the same wounds, desperately needing a role model and a "compensation father," and I met a clergyman or a Boy Scout leader or a Boys and Girls Club staffer or coach who could fill the bill — who wanted to fill the bill — it would never happen.

Why? Because adults who work with youth today have all attended one form or another of "sexual misconduct training." It's required by insurance providers. A more accurate title for the training might be "how not to get sued." Modern male youth workers (and it is men we're worried about, yes?) would never allow themselves to be alone with a child.

Oh sure, I get the party line: This new way of life is purported to keep our children safe, to make us more accountable, to raise the bar of our collective virtue, and to decrease the likelihood that the rest of us should ever have to face horrors similar to the recent traumas in the Catholic Church.

Yeah, I get it. But that doesn't stop me from thinking we've traded real character and real holiness for a holiness defined and written by insurance companies. Nor does it stop me from being grateful for meeting Rex before our great social institutions became so encumbered with wisdom and virtue.

Degrading, threatening children a too-frequent pastime

Did your parents ever call parts of your anatomy into the house, but not the rest of you? You know, you'd be out in the neighborhood talking to friends, the front door would open, and a voice would bellow, "Get your butt in here!"

I would shrug at my friends and say, "Gotta go; my dad wants to talk to my butt." I was tempted (but never had the courage) to walk bent over and backwards into the house, confront my father with my backside, look over my shoulder, wave, and say, "Sorry, Pops, the rest of me had to come, too."

Did you have parents who seemed a little confused about the actual role your bottom played in your childhood development and behavior? Who constantly attributed to your bottom influence in your life it did not deserve?

If you were, say, to clear the kitchen table and drop a plate on the floor, your mom or dad would blame your bottom. They would call your bottom "dumb." And, naturally, you would say, "My bottom didn't drop the plate; my hands dropped the plate." At which time your parents would call your bottom "smart."

To me, it seemed disingenuous. You can't have it both ways. Either my bottom is smart or it is dumb. And how would you give your derrière an I.Q. test anyway?

Maybe your folks would assign you some domestic task, and you were not thorough and complete in your work. Yep — they would blame that on your bottom. Specifically, they would complain that you only used half your bottom to do the job. You would apologize, of course, and promise that, next time, you would use your whole bottom.

If you were forgetful or negligent, if you failed to exercise common sense, or maybe weren't paying sufficient attention, many parents would actually share the same hallucination. They would look right at you and accuse you of something the finest vaudeville contortionist has never accomplished. It was a posture that would have made Gumby proud. My dad was fond of saying that, given how often I was in this supernatural posture, he was going to buy me a bathing cap to protect my hair.

Witty guy.

There are three reasons that television shows get cancelled: bad show, too much sex, or too much violence. If television critics and censors were ever privy to the dynamics of modern American parenting, a lot of families would be canceled. Parents can talk some serious violence:

I'm gonna beat your butt. I'm gonna blister your butt. (Like I said, the butt thing is really popular with parents.) I'm gonna slap you silly. (Hmm, brain damage as disciplinary intervention?) Wipe that smile off your face before I slap it off. I'm gonna knock you into next week. (You're gonna hit me so hard I'm gonna travel through time?) I'm gonna knock you into the next room. Do you want a spanking? (No, just a stern talking to, please.) I brought you into this world; I can take you out. (Okay, is it just me, or does murder sound like an overreaction to the bad behavior of your own progeny?)

Can you believe the permission parents give themselves to address their children in such degrading and disrespectful terms? To threaten their life and limb, even if rhetorically?

I mean, really. Can you believe it?

The Fifth Commandment (found in the oft-quoted Ten Commandments of the Hebrew Bible) is "Honor thy mother and father." I'm still looking for the biblical admonition "Dishonoring thy children is a terrific way to get them to behave honorably."

The day we became parents, we agreed that we could never, ever ask our children for any more respect than we were willing to extend. Which doesn't mean we've always been respectful to our children. It just means that we are just as accountable for our words, tones, and attitudes as our children.

Lucky for us, our children have so far been very forgiving. We're honored by their forgiveness.

A friend is loyal only to a friend's best interest

This is the story of Cathy and me, though you can be sure her name is not Cathy.

The room is full of seventh-graders, gathered to listen to me talk about Peer Intervention. In the next hour, I tell the students that, right now, somebody on this campus is in trouble. Maybe a bully. Maybe a drug or alcohol problem. Maybe a suicidal crisis. Maybe an exploitive or abusive adult. Despair. The potential for violence. Or self-destruction.

I tell the students that, if there is somebody on this campus in trouble, then I'm certain at least one other student knows about it. Because that's how it works. Adolescents in trouble tell somebody. They tell a peer. Then they apply a twisted definition of loyalty. They reveal the crisis and say, "Don't tell anybody."

I challenge the students to redefine loyalty. "Loyalty is one of friendship's highest attributes, yes," I tell them. "But we are never loyal to our friend; we are loyal to our friend's best interest." If our friend's best interest is best served by breaching our friend's confidence, then we do it. We break our promise to keep the secret. We tell someone. Right now.

A true friend flatly refuses to participate in your pathology. Every time.

I tell them that if they should find themselves at their friend's funeral after, say, a completed suicide, they will find zero consolation in thinking, "Well, at least I kept the secret just like he asked me to."

Class dismissed. I'm headed across the parking lot when I hear the teacher's voice calling behind me. Two girls have come to her, hardly moments after I leave the room. They want to talk to me.

The wide-eyed seventh-graders tell me about a peer. A girl, Cathy, who wears long-sleeved sweaters. They tell me what they saw under those sleeves.

I thank the girls, dismiss them, and we pull Cathy out of class. The teacher and I ask to see her arms.

It's a massacre. It's a zigzag of fresh wounds, healing wounds, and old white lines. My God. Her face is unaffected, detached, almost sublime. Her arms cry out as a diary. Tears come to my eyes.

Nutty enough, I think of a scene in William Peter Blatty's novel *The Exorcist* in which welts spontaneously form on the abdomen of young Regan, possessed these many days by a demon. The welts form the words "Help me." The welts are in Regan's handwriting.

Cathy writes her deeper psychic truth not with welts but with razor blades.

Without the two brave girls, I think Cathy would be dead today. Even then it was touch and go for the next eight months. I've never worked harder. Never felt less competent. Over my head. So helpless. Twice I tried to convince my supervisor that I should terminate therapy and refer this family. Twice my supervisor kicked my butt, and forced me to look at myself.

A professor of mine once said that, every so often, a patient would "getcha." That for reasons unclear and likely unconscious, a patient would come to mean something extraordinary to the therapist.

Cathy got me. I've got some cosmic Big Brother/Uncle/Guardian thing going on with her. I want her to make it.

Back in the days of my intellectual idolatry, I would now take off on a professorial, therapeutically correct lecture about counter-transference. I would objectify and analyze (read: discount and dismiss) the powerful bond that developed between this troubled girl and me.

Of course, counter-transference happens. And a healthy therapist is obliged to recognize it and manage it in a way that does not harm the patient. But I'm no longer willing to explain away the power, authenticity, and deep meaning of some therapeutic relationships. And part of their power lies in their reciprocity.

Transference, schmanference. Competent therapists aren't androids. We aren't vending machines. It's not skills that we bring to a session. We bring ourselves, and you should run terrified from any therapist who doesn't know that.

Fast forward a few years. I'm just east of the middle of nowhere in Utah. Today Cathy is graduated from a residential adolescent program. She asked me to come. I said only my own open-heart surgery could prevent me from being there.

Cathy is alive. The scars are gone or mostly faded. She's sober. Her eyes dance with life.

Score one for the good guys.

Beware the dangers of interrupting routine

The cool thing about routine is it sets you free to let your mind wander. You don't have to remember anything, because you'll recall whatever you need to recall when the time comes. You'll recall it because the routine has taught you that's where it belongs.

My friend asks me to recall a line from the third verse of a song I wrote. I stare at him like I have brain damage. If you threatened my life, I couldn't remember. And I wrote the song! So, he waits while I do the Rain Man murmur of the first verse . . . the second verse . . . the chorus . . . the middle-eight . . . the third verse . . . and there's the line he asked about. The routine made it appear like magic.

Be careful, though. If your routine gets interrupted, you can kill your children.

It's always been my job to take my son to daycare. From the time he was born. Every day I get up. Help the family get breakfast. My wife heads out with our two older sons and drives them to school. Convenient for her, because she works at that same school. I do the breakfast dishes, shower, and load up my little toddler snug in the car seat. His car seat is exactly where it belongs, in the back seat behind the driver. That's where he's the safest. From daycare, I drive to work.

That's my routine.

In May 1993, my wife interrupted my routine. She reminded me that my oldest son was starring in a jazz band concert at school. Why didn't I take my youngest to school, enjoy the concert, put the wee one back in the car, take him to daycare, and go to work from there?

So off I went to the school. The concert was fabulous. My oldest, a drummer, did a great job, and I was proud. My youngest motored around the back of the auditorium. I flirted with my wife. What a fun morning. Out to the parking lot. Little boy back in the car seat. Off I go.

Have I mentioned that my youngest is a boy who doesn't fuss much? Very self-contained. The zen of independent play. Never makes a peep in the car.

I probably forgot he was there in the first three hundred yards. He vanished into thin air because he had no place in the routine. My mind raced ahead into my work day — thinking, planning, organizing. I didn't drive to daycare. I drove right by daycare and straight to work. Pulled into the parking lot around eleven a.m. Parked in the bright sunshine. It was maybe ninety-four degrees and climbing.

I grab my valise. Off with the sunglasses and on with the spectacles. Quick glance around the car for CDs and cassettes. Can't be too careful. This Mojave Desert sun can quickly reduce your favorite music into mangled, melted plastic. Wouldn't want that to happen. Up. Out. Shut and lock door. A slight movement in the car catches my peripheral vision. I glance up to meet the innocent gaze of my then eighteen-month-old staring at me through the passenger window.

If I had not leaned against the car, I would have collapsed to the asphalt. Heart pounding. I can barely breathe. Right now there's an alternative future veering away in which EMTs and police officers are surrounding my car, pronouncing my son dead at the scene.

I give serious thought to keeping the whole thing to myself, but in the end I tell the boy's mother. I made myself memorize the sick look on her face. Don't kid yourself. Good, normal, intelligent, regular folks can find themselves planning a child's funeral for no other reason than because their routines were interrupted.

We're that vulnerable.

A Father's Day challenge: Be a better role model

My favorite movie of all time is *To Kill a Mockingbird*. I watch it once or twice a year. I practically have the dialogue memorized. I get choked up in the same four spots each time. The innocence of the little girl Jean Louise "Scout" disarms me. The boyishness, imagination, and fierce pride of Scout's older brother Jem reminds me of me. The soundtrack provokes pensive melancholy, but a kind of melancholy that feels familiar, solid, and right, like the memory of things holy, painful, and heroic.

But mostly I want Atticus Finch to be my father.

Atticus is a widower with a young son and daughter. He is a lawyer living in the Depression-era Deep South. The county judge asks Atticus to defend a black man accused of raping a white woman. Atticus takes the case.

His first-grade daughter, Scout, is hot-headed and loyal. When a classmate taunts Scout about her father's advocacy for a black man, Scout responds with playground fisticuffs. Her father finds her at home, suspended from school, chagrined, confused, and angry.

"Atticus, do you defend niggers?" Scout asks.

"Don't say 'nigger,' Scout," is her father's troubled reply. "I'm simply defending a Negro, Tom Robinson. There's been some high talk around town to the effect that I shouldn't do much about defending this man."

"If you shouldn't be defending him, then why are you doing it?" Scout asks.

Atticus ponders the question, and says, "For a number of reasons. The main one is that if I didn't, I couldn't hold my head up in town. I couldn't even tell you or Jem not to do something again."

Atticus doesn't turn philosophical and begin some soliloquy about how all men are created equal. Atticus doesn't turn moral judge, and discuss how pathetic is the ignorance of racism. He doesn't turn bleeding heart social worker. He doesn't self-congratulate regarding his superior enlightenment. He doesn't see himself as being in possession of a better spirituality or religion.

He is simply a prisoner to the voice of his own integrity. And, in that sense, you could even say he is self-serving. He wants to be able to hold his head up in town. He wants to retain his moral authority to be a father and good disciplinarian. He is willing to risk his own social reputation to be able to say he was true to himself. What he doesn't know, of course, is that his commitment to his integrity will ultimately cost him more than public reputation. The lives of Atticus' children will ultimately be threatened, too.

Atticus loses the local trial. The courtroom clears, except for the upstairs galley, where local blacks have been segregated and Jem and Scout have watched the trial. The Negro community quietly stands in honor and gratitude for the integrity of Atticus Finch.

"Miss Jean Louise," says the kind Baptist preacher. "Stand up. Your father's passing."

Bob Ewell, the father of the alleged rape victim, isn't satisfied with winning a guilty verdict against an innocent black man nor that man's panicked escape attempt wherein he is shot to death. No; Bob resolves to get drunk and attempt to murder Atticus' children. He succeeds in breaking Jem's arm before running into some difficulties. Arthur "Boo" Radley, a developmentally disabled adult, himself a life-long victim of vicious social prejudice, a heretofore recluse, decides to act with integrity, too. Which, in this case, means intercepting the attempted murder by shoving a kitchen knife under Bob's ribs. Life is pretty simple for Boo.

The doctor sets Jem's arm. The local sheriff, disgusted with recent events, and perhaps disgusted with himself, too, doctors the record and officially concludes that Bob Ewell fell on his knife. The dead bury the dead.

An adult Jean Louise Finch narrates the film in retrospect, and describes her father's vigil over her unconscious, injured brother: "He would be in Jem's room all night. And he would be there when Jem waked up in the morning."

Happy Father's Day, dads. I figure you'll have lots of people supporting your entitlement to relaxation and pampering and affirmation today, so I'm taking a different tack. I'm going to put some pressure on you. Turn up the burner.

Do I have to tell you? Every day, every moment, your sons and daughters are watching you. Taking notes in their souls. Looking for cues. Learning. Digesting. And when you pass, down the hallway or from this life, will there be something about you that compels them to stand?

Father-son bond strengthened through gun education

I find myself at American Shooter's World in Las Vegas. This is my fiftieth Christmas on planet Earth, and I have never been in a gun shop until right now. My ignorance of firearms is comprehensive. Categorical.

I didn't get the gun gene. Guns make me feel girly and stupid. I'm not anti-gun, though I confess to being vociferously anti-macho idiot with gun. I just never got into hunting, target shooting, or blowing stuff up in the desert on a Sunday afternoon.

Which is weird, because I grew up in the Golden Age of Westerns. The television of my boyhood was swimming in guns and gunfire. Roy Rogers, *Gunsmoke*, *Bonanza*, *The Rifleman*, *Wild, Wild West*, *Alias Smith and Jones*, *Have Gun Will Travel* — geez. According to *TV Guide*, there was no problem the right gun couldn't solve.

I learned to make my hand into the gun shape nearly before I learned to wave. And the gun sound! Yeah — you cough air up from your throat, bounce it off the palate, using the cheeks and lips for vibrato. (One of the perplexing mysteries of childhood was why it was impossible to teach a girl to make the gun noise.) With each gun noise, you depress your thumb over the index finger of your gun-shaped hand. Mow your friends down.

I'm proud to say I was once thrown out of my high school library for participating in a pantomime gunfight. I beat Keith to the draw, sending him mortally wounded over the back side of a couch. But I didn't see Carl hiding behind the magazine rack, who shot me dead on the spot. Students applauded.

Wouldn't recommend this prank in a post-Columbine world.

But somehow I was never drawn into the world of actual guns. As a father, I had to make a decision about home self-defense. I made my decision weighing two worst-case scenarios: 1) I watch helplessly as murderous intruder kills member of my family, or 2) my son finds my home defense weapon and kills himself or his brother.

I decided not to own a gun.

My eighth-grade son? He got the gun gene! (Must have passed down from the mother.) He digs blowing stuff up. He is wide-eyed about guns. Mesmerized. That's why I'm at Shooter's World. I'm Christmas shopping for my beautiful manly man thirteen-year-old.

I'm greeted by Salesman Mike. Mike's head is shaved. He's a body-builder. His wardrobe is pure testosterone. Black shirt, pants, commando boots. Navy Seal meets S.W.A.T. joined by Marine Special Forces with a dash of Ninja Turtle. Yikes.

But it all changes when Mike shakes my hand and smiles. I recognize that smile. Warm. Infectious. Generous. Joyful. It's my boy as a man. Mike and my son are cosmic kin.

Mike spends an unhurried hour with me. Crash course education. Mike shows me how I can grant my son this experience while allowing me peace of mind. It's a triple system of redundancy. The trigger lock makes it unfireable. The magazine lock makes it unloadable. And only I have possession of the keys and the ammo.

I can live with that.

But Mike is not merely generous with his knowledge; he is generous with his life, too. He tells me stories of his father and his brothers. Stories of pride in a military heritage. Memories of hunting trips. His gratitude for the respect his father communicated to him through high expectations, discipline, and an insistence upon responsibility.

This is what really sells me. Why would I want to hide the fact of guns from my boy when a gun education provides the chance to teach so many good things? And let me be perfectly and shamelessly selfish here: I want my son to talk about me someday the way Mike talks about his dad. Of course no father/son relationship is without injuries and estrangements. But the abiding reality in Mike's stories is mutual respect, gratitude, and admiration.

I covet that. I value those things.

It was my boy's lot in life to have a father who is a poet, dreamer, wordsmith, songwriter, orator, and philosopher. To his father fell the fortune of a son who is all boy.

Under the Christmas tree my boy finds a Marine-issue Mossberg 590 pump shotgun. His grin alters the course of comets light years away.

We're going to take a gun safety course together. Then we're going to go blow some stuff up.

Together.

Corporal punishment does more harm than good

My friend and his four-year-old get into a van with another dad and his young son. The second boy is complaining. Talks back. His father reaches to the back seat and pops the boy on the naked thigh with an open hand. Whap! My friend's boy takes notice. His eyes blaze: "Don't you hit him!"

The man is stunned. Contemplates his pint-sized accuser for a moment. Turns slowly to my friend and says, "Let me guess. You don't hit your kids."

My friend shrugs, almost self-consciously. "Why would I want to hit him?"

It's an excellent question. Corporal punishment is a cultural prejudice, and particularly a Euro-American prejudice. There have been and still are cultures all over this planet where it's unheard of to strike children in any manner as a strategy for education or character formation.

Does corporal punishment work? Depends on your definition of "work." Can it garner a kind of compliance? Sometimes. However, it's just as likely to provoke defiance and deception, not to mention its cost in trust, respect, and affection.

I have three sons. Their mother and I decided upon an experiment of sorts. Was it necessary to hit children to turn them into good people and productive adults? What would become of children who were never spanked or slapped, let alone struck with paddles, spoons, coat hangers, fly swatters, or other household weapons? We decided not to hit them.

I didn't say I never wanted to hit them. Ooh baby. I was holding my second son on the second day of his life. My twenty-two-month-old first-born was playing with a metal Matchbox car. He toddled over to stare at his new baby brother. "Hi, Jonathan! This is Aaron," I said, basking in the dear little family moment. Whereupon Jonathan reared back and hurled the Matchbox car in our direction. It hit me on the bridge of the nose, bringing blood. To this day I'm not sure if Jonathan, newly deposed from his Kingdom of the Only Child, was aiming at me or the little usurper in my arms.

Oh yeah. My first reaction was powerful, angry, and violent. I spun the chair around and hollered for mom: "Get Jonathan away from me!" And she did. In the fantasy, however, I put the baby down and lay my hands on my boy. I hit back. I actually entertain the idea that I, a 6-foot-1, 180-pound man, have a physical score to settle with a toddler weighing hardly more than a Thanksgiving turkey.

And I didn't say our experiment in child-rearing was without a few setbacks. Their mom and I each filed one demerit — she when she intercepted Jonathan tipping over the bassinet of his two-week-old brother and gave our eldest a wop on his diapered can, and me when a three-year-old Joseph punched me square in the nose. In one preconscious reaction I lowered him from my arms and gave him two shots to his backside while shouting, "Don't you ever hit me!" Yep, yours truly once spent seven seconds on this planet thinking that hitting my youngest son would be a terrific strategy for teaching him not to hit.

I won't blame you if you need to take a little break from reading this column to let the irony sink in. It's right up there on the Moron Scale with hitting children to get them to stop crying.

See, the thing is, so much of corporal punishment is just that — a preconscious reaction to fear and anger. In the absence of fear and anger — that is, when parents are rational — corporal punishment becomes silly and unnecessary.

Unless, of course, you believe deeply in corporal punishment as ritual and ceremony. A quiet, rational use of absolute power. Go to your room and wait for me. Go get the paddle. Come over here and bend over my knee. Grab your ankles. Pull down your pants and bend over. We invite our children to humiliate and degrade themselves without protest, and we tell ourselves we are teaching obedience.

Oh, we're teaching something all right. We're teaching self-loathing.

And please don't start with "The Bible says 'spare the rod, spoil the child.'" The rod mentioned in the Hebrew scripture is the rod used for sheepherding. Look it up. Ever watch Middle Eastern sheepherders? They walk behind the sheep, tapping them on the flank to steer and guide them.

But Semitic sheepherders don't beat their sheep. Sheep aren't bright enough to make the connection between the pain of the blows and the desired correction of behavior. This proverb is about a child's need for guidance, monitoring, and boundaries, not a divine authorization to hit children.

Stop hitting your children. Stop now.

We usually know when it's time to go home

In the summer of 1970, you would have found me sardined into a station wagon with my mom, my dad, my two sisters, lots of luggage, and an Etch-a-Sketch, on our way from Phoenix, Arizona to Yellowstone National Park. My older sister could write naughty words with the Etch-a-Sketch. I was impressed.

My siblings and I played tag-team car sickness the whole way and back again. My dad used to say that the one silver lining in having a car that reeked of bile was it made short work of the border guard search when we came home from vacations in Mexico. The guard would open the hatchback, stick his head in, freeze, withdraw his head quickly, and pronounce our car good to go. Good thing, too, because our car was usually carrying heavy ordinance of Mexican fireworks and the occasional undeclared bottle of tequila.

My special interest as a boy was the curio shop: tiny spoons with state logos, letter openers, scorpions entombed in acrylic paperweights, polished rocks, my name on a refrigerator magnet, rubber knives, gag buzzers. The preeminent glory of capitalism in America might just be its genius ability to manufacture and make us buy absolute crap. Cat litter has more intrinsic value than the average highway souvenir.

We fished in Idaho. We saw all the cool geothermal stuff — geysers and "hot pots." We beheld the mountains. We saw bears and bison and eagles and elk; Yellowstone had yet to reintroduce the gray wolf to the environment. We spent all my parents' money. We saw and did all there was to see and do.

Then my father announced it was time to go home.

My little sister cried. I became sullen and obnoxious. We begged to stay a few more days. And darned if my parents didn't put us in the car and drive home anyway.

At some point during the trek home, I woke up in the back seat. It was quiet. Dark. Highway signs rolling by. My mother reached over and patted my father's leg. "It will be good to get home," she said.

And she was right. It was good to get back to the familiar routine and the home-cooked meals. It was good to be home.

This is the image that rushes back to me now as I sit and talk to the ninety-five-year-old woman. She is old. Her skin is like rice paper. If I sit too close, her hearing aid feeds back with a high-pitched whine. If I sit too far away, she can't see me. Her dentures, ill-fitted around aged gums, click and pop as she speaks.

Her body has betrayed her, she says with a smile. Her eyes have seen more than thirty thousand sunsets. Her ears heard Franklin Roosevelt's voice pouring live out of her radio, declaring war on Japan. Her immigrant grandparents died in the Great Chicago Fire. Her first rotary dial telephone had a four-digit phone number. She thinks McDonald's is a fine restaurant.

She's ready to die, and she tells me so. In fact, that's why I'm here. The old woman is frustrated with her closest family members, because they won't let her talk about dying. "They keep telling me that I can't give up, that I'm going to be okay," she says. "Look at me!" She lifts her arms in comic incredulity. "Does it look like I'm going to be okay?" Her laughter is the phlegm wheeze of an exhaling tee kettle left on a cooling stove top.

She's tired. She hurts all the time. Her peers are all dead. She misses her husband, gone these last twenty-five years. She has buried one daughter lost to cancer. She sees the modern world swallowing up the time and energies of her grandchildren and great-granchildren.

She's not angry with God, but definitely impatient. She's like an airline traveler whose plane had been delayed — sitting, surrounded by luggage, packed and ready to go, but no way to get there. And when you ask at the desk for an estimated time of departure, they just shrug their shoulders. We'll let you know.

She talks of heaven.

I notice I'm feeling sorry for her family members. They are missing this conversation. It's a big deal to be invited into a human being's mortality. It's beyond intimate. Sacred, even.

She's not suicidal. She loves life. No; her words are the words of a weary vacation traveler. She has spent all her money. She has seen and done all there is to see and do. She leans her head back against the rocker with a half-smile and knows that it will be good to get home.

Male and Female Matters

IF IT WASN'T FOR OUR SEX DRIVE — OUR ATTRACTION AND DESIRE FOR THE OTHER — SOMETIMES I THINK MEN AND WOMEN WOULD LIVE ON SEPARATE CONTINENTS. We're that different.

And it's not just objective and measurable differences; it's differences that alienate, or at least always have the potential to alienate. Men and women are, on some level, alien to each other. Every time a man and woman join in friendship or fall in love, they are on some level attempting to heal and reconcile an archetypal estrangement.

This mystery, this canyon gap between the sexes, is universally recognizable even in our post-feminist culture, which tries so hard to pretend those differences are mere learned prejudice.

Not so. The differences are real. They delight us, perplex us, aggravate us, compel us, repulse us, make us crazy. He's my hero. She's a goddess. Men are selfish. Women are controlling. He's my protector. She's so nurturing. He's valiant. She's virtuous. He's a pig. She's a whore.

See, all those things are true. Simultaneously. Trouble is, until men and women find health and wholeness of self, each tends to see the other in caricature. Pieces and parts. Distortions and projections. Sexism is an equal-opportunity temptation. Men and women idealize one another. Then they vilify one another. Neither view is whole or accurate. Or helpful.

Men and women each wield their own disproportion of power. Men have more physical strength. Women have more sexual power. Men rule the world of logic and analysis. Women have the advantage in wisdom and synthesis. Whoever coined the maxim, "You can't see the forest for the trees" was undoubtedly a women talking to a man. Lost to history, of course, was the masculine retort, "That may well be, but I'm much less likely to walk *into* a tree while walking through the forest."

Each is afraid of the other's power, and with good reason. A subtext of all male/female relationships is this suspicion, this mistrust, this negotiation of our respective vulnerabilities and reciprocal ambivalence and antipathy.

The ancient Hebrews saw some essential estrangement between the genders that required healing. It's reflected in the Hebrew Myth of Adam and Eve, the original man and woman (see Genesis, Chapter 1-3). In innocence, Adam and Eve "stood together naked and were not ashamed." Then Sin corrupts the world, and "he shall rule over you, yet your desire shall be for him."

That a man could want or need to rule over a woman says something has gone terribly wrong. That a woman could want to have sex with a man who wants to rule over her boggles the mind. It's a tragedy. An ancient wound that begs for healing.

A date and I introduce our mutual friend to a woman. A well-intentioned matchmaking effort. Drinks. An appetizer. It is going well. Until the bar patron with the terrifying breast augmentation walks by. Stifled laughs around the table. I cup my mouth and feign to shout "Heellloooo" and then turn my ear as if to hear the echo that might emanate from the mountain slopes of silicone. My friend says if he falls in there, would we please toss in a flashlight so he can find his way out. My date makes some remark about beach balls.

Snort. Giggle. Suppressed laughter. Until we turn to look into the stone face of this woman. My mirth freezes in mid-chuckle. "Let me guess," I say, wincing. "You don't think this is very funny."

Her reproving gaze doesn't waver. "I think it's a guy thing," she says, bathing me in patient condescension.

Our mutual friend ponders her response for a moment, shrugs, and offers back, "I don't know. Could be just a real uptight woman thing."

She gasps. Collects her coat and purse. Leaves. Our friend turns to us and says, "I don't think she's my soul mate."

Like I said, there's a mystery between the genders that always threatens to alienate. It's the stuff of television sitcoms. It's fodder for every stand-up comedy act since the dawn of stand-up comedy. We can laugh about it, or cry. The people I know in thriving love affairs learn to laugh about it, often and loudly. Bemusement and satire are important friends to great male/female relationships. Intimate couples tease each other relentlessly.

Healthy men and women love being men and women, respectively. Healthy men love women to be women. Healthy women love men to be men. Neither apologizes for selfhood nor has much occasion to criticize the other. Each would miss in the other even those parts that make our eyes roll and provoke sighs of vexed exasperation. "What is it with women!?" . . . "Isn't that just like a man!"

Yeah? What's your point?

For some, the struggle yields growth and maturity, a strength of self that can relinquish fear and prejudice and behold the other in mystery and admiration. There emerges a respect sometimes joyful, sometimes begrudging, but respect nonetheless. In friendship, each provides the other a balance. In emotionally committed love relationships, each coaxes the other toward the goal of standing naked, yet not ashamed.

Taking off your clothes is the easy part of being naked.

Superhero myths reveal man's struggle with power, intimacy

My youngest son is four years old, and his every waking moment is steeped in superheroes. Superman, Batman, Spider-Man — he has all the costumes and has virtually memorized all the movies.

"Good morning, Joseph," I'll say.

"Look again," he'll say. "My name is not Joseph."

I'll turn around and, sure enough, there's Batman. Or at least a four-year-old boy in a Batman mask, shirt, cape, maybe or maybe not Batman underwear, and his mother's stiletto heeled boots. Seems Batman occasionally forgets his pants. Batman meets the Village People.

Once he came downstairs in the Spider-Man mask, the Batman shirt, and the Superman cape and belt. Called himself Super Spiderbat. Criminals didn't stand a chance.

When I was a boy, I wasn't privy to all these cool costumes. Not a problem. All I needed was a kitchen dish towel and some masking tape for a makeshift cape. The remaining details all happened in my imagination. I would beat up the bad guys and save the world.

Or I would strap on my cap gun six-shooters and be the Lone Ranger. The neighbor boy next door would be my sidekick, Tonto. His little sister would be The Girl in Big Trouble. She kept messing up the plot by asking for a gun, and we would have to explain to her time and again that girls don't carry guns. Just scream for help until the Lone Ranger and Tonto come to save you. Then thank us and cook dinner. Or something.

It didn't occur to me until my adulthood what so many of these superheroes had in common: anonymity and isolation. They often had secret identities or, if not, kept very much to themselves. They could rescue babies and children, but could never really have relationships with them. And women? Sheesh. They could be attracted to women (see upside-down Spider-Man being kissed by the Kirsten Dunst character clad in clingy, rain-wet T-shirt), or even love them (see Batman and Catwoman), but never in reciprocal relationship *with* them.

The mind-boggling powers of superheroes, it seems, can withstand just about anything except recognition and relationship. Kryptonite is a minor inconvenience compared to the threat of being known and loved for oneself.

Superheroes cannot even hang around long enough to tolerate gratitude. By the time you'd collected yourself and turned to thank Tarzan for killing the marauding lion, he'd melted back into the jungle. "That is his way," the tribal native would explain. As a boy, I thought this elusive masculine mystique was cool. As a man, I think

Tarzan's "way" is wussy. He can defend our vulnerability, yet never extend his own. When it came to life's biggest challenge — human intimacy — Tarzan used mystique to disguise cowardice.

In *Superman II*, Lois Lane discovers Clark Kent's identity as Superman. She says, "I'm in love with you." He goes to his North Pole headquarters to talk to his virtual reality mom about love, sex, and women. "This is the question we had hoped you would never ask," is Virtual Mom's reply. She says that if Superman is to be in a relationship with Lois, he has to become mortal like Lois. Ergo, Superman has to make a choice between his power and intimacy. He can't have both.

Superman surrenders his powers. He and Lois have a romp. Bad guys come to Earth. All hell breaks loose. Superman regrets his decision to be known by Lois, regains his powers, and kicks butt. Then, at the end of the film, we see a weeping Lois coming to grips with the limits of the relationship. She understands that she can never truly embrace the love between them.

Actually it's worse than that. Because now Superman erases her memory. If he is to be Superman, he can't even tolerate her *memory* of their intimacy.

"Pay no attention to the man behind the curtain," says another superhero of sorts, the Wizard of Oz. But Dorothy does pay attention. And thank heavens, for until we meet someone who insists on looking behind the curtain, us guys don't stand a chance of ever becoming truly human.

"You're a very bad man," Dorothy scolds the wizard.

No, Dorothy. A very frightened man.

Men, women have built-in communication preferences

A reader writes: "**[The subject of sex has caused a conflict between my partner and me. She said] I 'cheapened' it by talking about it directly. . . . How could telling somebody that I want to have sex with her cheapen the act of doing it? Should I better speak in implication, and refer to sex or her attributes indirectly? Well, how do I do that, and *why* should I have to?**"

All right, first the prejudicial "guy" answer:

Women decide. They know when and how it's okay to talk about sex, and when and how it's okay to have sex. And you'll never know how they decide. Because it's a secret. And it changes. On a bright Tuesday afternoon you can openly admire the way she looks in those jeans, and she'll shoot you a siren grin and give you a toss of her beautiful hair. Make a similar comment four days later, and you get a lecture about how you're objectifying her and how come all you ever talk about is sex.

(Here all guys stand and cheer.)

But maybe we should dig deeper. What's going on here? Why do so many men experience women this way?

I observe three things:

- Biological differences: Men and women are different. Their brains are different. Their psychosexuality is different. The research is clearer than ever about this. The female sex drive is wired more to the epidermis; the male sex drive is jump-started more often visually. There is truth in the generalization that, when women feel connected, they want to have sex. Men want to have sex so they can feel connected.

  My prejudice is that a fair number of women misspeak themselves when they chastise their mates regarding direct sexual invitations. I think they're trying to find a way to say, "I don't yet feel connected. . . . I don't have a context for this." Because, once connected, healthy women love men to be men. They can and do enjoy a balanced proportion of their man's unvarnished, very direct — sometimes coarse — courtship.

- Social vulnerabilities: Pregnancy creates disproportionate economic and physical vulnerabilities for women. Apart from that, men are typically bigger and stronger than women. Her risk in sexual courtship is more immediate. More urgent. There are some very rational reasons for her to approach this courtship with a need to rehearse respect and safety. This need is often miscommunicated as a begrudging or "put-down" of the mas-culine. An *a priori* chip on her shoulder. A defensiveness.

- Acculturation: Western civilization tends to raise women with the prejudice that a "real lady" approaches the subject of her own sexuality inferentially and indirectly, sometimes to the point of denial. And a woman in denial or ashamed of her own sex drive has a way of projecting harsh opinions about the masculine sex drive. That same culture tends to raise men to be very conscious and intentional about sexuality, to the point of aggrandizement. It's a shame really, both for men and women, that our culture so often peddles these distorted images of male and female.

My ideal courtship? That a man and woman would practice an artful balance. The man would learn and patiently practice the cer-emonies of connection — cards, conversation, rose petals, candles, nuance, clean sheets, unhurried touch. And he would do this for no other reason than because she likes it and feels loved because of it. Along the way, he also might learn to enjoy the beauty of it for its own sake.

The woman would learn to value — even if not prefer — her man's uncensored desire. She would learn and practice the art of direct initiation. And she would do this for no other reason than because he likes it and feels loved because of it. Along the way, she also might learn to enjoy the raw passion of it for its own sake.

In the meantime, here's a metaphor: In the South, you go to your neighbor's house to borrow a cup of sugar while pretending you just dropped by. Both you and your neighbor know full well you did not merely drop by. Yet the pretense is not phony; it's ceremonial. It's a ceremony that allows for the strengthening of respect and safety. It's a script. Beautiful, really. Makes people less likely to feel used or taken for granted.

Follow the script consistently, and your neighbor just might give you a house key.

I'm trying to be subtle. Give you a house key. Get it?

Why do women always fall for the bad boys?

The knock comes to my graduate school dorm room in Dallas, Texas, on a Friday night around 11:30. She's a friend in tears. She proceeds to inform me she has just now left her date sitting in her dorm room next door.

"He keeps pressuring me for sex, and I don't want to have sex on the first date," she says.

"So don't have sex with him," I say.

"I told him that," she says. "And he got all mad. He said he drove here all the way from Plano, took me to dinner, took me to a movie, and . . ."

She is starting to remind me of Hamlet.

"So, what are we talking here?" I say. "Ten dollars in gas, throw in five for the wear and tear on the vehicle, did you say fifty-five for dinner, twelve for the movie and another twelve for concessions . . . we talking not quite one hundred dollars for the evening? And he paid for everything, right?"

"Yeah," she whimpers, nodding.

"So, for one hundred dollars, he's thinks he's entitled to sex with you?"

"Yeah," she nods again.

The penny won't drop. This proverbial penny is fatally jammed in the mechanism. Drastic measures are required: "Is that how much you normally charge for sex?"

Now the penny drops. The whole piggy bank, in fact. "That #$!%$!," she says between her teeth. She stands tall, shoulders square. "Thank you," she says, and strides out of the room. Her head bobs past my window. I step outside and look toward her dormitory.

Suddenly a shrill female voice. Then a deeper male voice. More shrill. Something slams. The door opens and out comes a shoe. Then another shoe. Then a coat. Then a very unhappy guy. He collects his wardrobe and fades into the parking lot.

Note to guy: It's always a red flag when your date says, "Excuse me just a minute, I have to go next door and talk to my therapist."

When I was in college, guys tended to fall into two groups. There were jerks, and there were gentlemen. And it was a well-known fact among us gentlemen: The jerk gets the girl. Every time.

What is it with women and bad boys? Aloof. Unavailable. Unreliable. Treat women like crap. Sexually entitled. Selfish and primitive in bed. Hubba, hubba. Give me more of that! What's the allure? Why do women stand in line to turn these guys' heads and win the chance to be ravaged and then ignored? I'm not making fun. I'm really asking.

Tom Lykus is a radio personality hosting *The Tom Lykus Show.* Four p.m. Monday through Friday, 1140-AM here in Las Vegas. He calls himself The Professor. He teaches guys to treat women badly. He says guys can have more sex more often with more women if they will be inattentive, unavailable, and generally self-centered. The jerk gets the girl.

And Lykus is right. Exaggerated? Grossly. Contemptuous? Uh-huh. Sophomoric and boorish? Absolutely. But the only way this radio show is this popular (and, frankly, this funny) is because it has its arms wrapped around an observable truth.

The observable truth? We tend to raise women in this culture with an insufficient sense of self. These same women, then, in adolescence and early adulthood, often look for that self — and ultimately have that self swallowed up — in pursuit of a man's attention. But not just any man. Gentlemen are boring. Bad boys are the real challenge. Ooo baby.

Greg Behrendt and Liz Tuccillo co-authored the best-selling book *He's Just Not That Into You.* Funny, funny, funny — until you get done reading it and get done laughing. Then it hits you. This is pathetic. Here are the actual chapter titles: He's just not that into you if he . . . is not asking you out, not calling you, not dating you, not having sex with you, having sex with someone else, only wants to see you when he's drunk, doesn't want to marry you, breaking up with you, has disappeared on you, is married, is a selfish jerk, a bully, or a really big freak.

No way this book is a best-seller unless there is a significant number of women out there who read these items as epiphany.

The most popular song from my last CD is "I'll Wash Your Lover's Car." I often introduce it on stage by saying, "This song is dedicated to women I've known for whom no amount of data ever leads to the conclusion 'He's a jerk and I should leave him.'" And then people chuckle and love the song. But, for all the song's tongue-in-cheek, I fear that nobody gets it.

I'm being serious.

Neither gentleman nor jerk is the right approach

A few months ago I wrote a column about the penchant of some women for dating "bad boys." I said that, while in college, it seemed us guys quickly fell into two types: gentlemen and jerks. And it was a well-known fact among us gentlemen that the jerk gets the girl. Every time.

The column focused on my clinical prejudice that this culture tends to raise women with an insufficient sense of self. Many American women, then, go through a stage somewhere between eighteen and as late as forty when they seek that self through compulsive, vicarious, and often unhappy bonds with unavailable men.

Jerks come in various forms and flavors, but the common denominator is that they are unavailable. They'll take what you give them, even for a time make a woman feel terrific about the giving (Oh, yes, he wants to use *me!*) But his signature is unavailability. Reciprocal vulnerability and real presence are never part of the deal.

The column bemoaned how those women would befriend us gentlemen, admire us, trust us, even call us at three a.m. to vent about how The Jerk they went home with last night treated them like (surprise!) a jerk. But they wouldn't date us. They didn't desire us. Some would flat out say it: "You're too nice."

Yet, even as I wrote the column, I knew the story wasn't complete. I promised myself I'd follow up. So here it is:

The Gentleman is not always what he seems to be. He's left half his game in the locker room. I'm saying some men use the persona of "gentlemen" because they are not entirely honest with themselves or the woman they seek to court.

The Gentleman thinks of women as poetry. He thinks of the Goddess. To approach her, he "softens" himself. He cloaks his naturally hard-edge, primitive masculinity with the persona of Nice Guy. He dotes. Pays attention. Listens. Moi? Thinking about taking you home and turning you every which way but loose? Never! I want to hear more about your career and childhood.

The Gentleman prides himself by putting women on a pedestal. Treats them as works of art. Fragile glass. He's tender. Empathic. Unavailable? Sheesh. He's omni-available. You'll practically be tripping over him.

Now, I wish I had a dime for every woman I've ever met who has protested, "Are you kidding? How can I meet a guy like that? I would think I'd died and gone to heaven!" And then I wish I had another dime for how many times that same woman would eventually grow bored, begin to see those same attributes as weak, soft, too nice. She dumps him. Or worse, stays, with nothing to offer but quiet (or not-so-quiet) disdain.

I'm gonna die saying the mark of a healthy women is that she LOVES a man to be a man. All of a man. Even those parts that irritate her and make her roll her eyes and sigh. It's the immutable differences that make her crazy for him.

A friend changed my life when he said, "Steven, you know why we put people on pedestals? To get them out of the way!"

The Gentleman uses chivalry and gentility and empathy for all the wrong reasons. The persona of gentleman is for some men an unconscious defense. It gives them an excuse to put off the rigorous work of embracing a deeper masculinity. It keeps women at bay, even as it deigns to revere those same women.

Healthy women don't like being idealized. Too much pressure. Pedestals are lonely, boring places. Even occasionally deadly. (Just ask Marilyn Monroe.) Healthy women feel the distance idealization creates. It's not real. Not earthy enough.

It's not love.

They are just women after all.

I'm saying that the Gentleman needs to stop whining and take some responsibility. Maybe he's being dishonest with himself. Sometimes "gentleman" is a ruse. A disguise for fear. Of course she's not attracted to us.

In the end, the Gentleman and the Jerk need to go have a beer together. Chat. Become acquainted. Alone, they are sad caricatures of manhood. Together, they might make one studly dude.

Sexual harassment is more complicated than just sex

It was in the mid-'90s when I attended my first mandatory "Sexual Harassment Prevention Training" at my place of business. I was the supervisor of eleven therapists whose specialty was prevention psychology. All of us trouped into the conference room to learn how not to harass one another sexually. Three hours it took me to teach us how not to degrade, disrespect, or exploit one another sexually.

(So, like, it's wrong to snap the exposed band of someone's underwear? Can we use the word "navel" in a sentence?)

I don't mean to make light. Sexual harassment, especially in relationships of unequal power, is grotesque. It should be against the law. It's just that the way we go about remedying the phenomenon is patronizing and ineffective.

At least my team of therapists thought so. They spent the three hours trying to listen and act professional, but unable to resist passing notes back and forth and snickering. Some might say it was nervous laughter, but I thought it was more like offended laughter. When I hold something in contempt, or when I'm offended by something, I cannot stop the part of my brain that simply *must* lampoon the object of my contempt.

Actually Barbara beat me to the punch. Barbara was a member of my staff. Barbara was my friend. I stepped out of the conference room on to the front sidewalk where my troops had gathered. "Whaddya think of the training?" I asked Barbara. She turned, smiled bright, whacked me on my rump, and said, "Nice job!"

Gales of laughter. Folks weeping. Doubled over. The team was never closer. People had never felt safer or more trusting of each other and me.

The issue in sexual harassment is never sex. The issue has to do with the consciousness and integration of the people involved, which is to say their relative psychological maturity. For example:

Two women stand at the office copier. A male colleague stops to chat. His conversation includes a joke with sexual double-entendre. Hah-hah-hah. The air among these three is warm and safe. Each goes back to his or her desk lighter. There's a sense of recreation and celebration.

That afternoon, same two women at the copier. A different male colleague pauses. Tells a similar joke. This time the ladies don't laugh. The air is tense, stiff, hostile. Within the hour, the man is sitting in front of a supervisor being written up and disciplined for sexual harassment.

What's the difference between the two men? The difference is the consciousness and integration of their sexual selves. The first man knows who he is, knows his desires and his passions, knows when he's attracted to someone, and because he knows he can make decisions about it that serve the best interest of collegiality and friendship. He can "read" the level of trust and rapport between himself and other women, and he knows when sexual content will be playful and tension breaking, rather than unwanted and tension producing.

The second man is both blind to himself and blind to the fact that he is blind to himself. Rather than possess a conscious sexuality about which he can make conscious decisions, he leaks it. People tend to not like it when you leak sexual energy on them.

Bram Stoker's novel, *Dracula*, written at the height of the puritanical Victorian Era, is, oddly enough, not about vampires. It's a story about what happens when men cannot or will not live consciously with their sexuality. If a man is raised with the idea that his sexuality is something terrible and shameful, he will cut it off from his consciousness. It will then hide during the day, rising only at night. It will dominate the will of the masculine.

And suck the life out of the feminine.

Masculinity defies a simple definition

In couples therapy, competent therapists don't take sides — or so they say. In truth, we take sides all the time, it's just that we usually do so in the privacy of our own mind. We're trained to keep our opinions cloaked. Objectivity is our signature calling card.

But it's unavoidable. I can't help forming opinions as I listen to husbands and wife recount their grievances with each other.

Which is why the couple in front of me intrigues. Their debate has me stumped. I don't mean professionally. I mean personally. I don't take sides — out loud or privately — not because I'm too cool and professional to do so, but because I don't have an opinion about which I'm confident.

Their fifteen-year-old is off to an amusement park in California with his schoolmates. There's this roller-coaster ride where you sit on something similar to a ski lift, your legs dangling in the air. Then you rocket through the air, up and down, sideways, corkscrew, loop-de-loop. Pretty sure you scream the whole time.

The boy is afraid. His personality has always been intense, pensive — very sensitive. He has never liked guns or loud cars or horror movies. At his first trip to Disneyland, age eight, he much preferred the shooting gallery and Swiss Family Robinson Tree House to The Matterhorn or The Haunted House. He got through Pirates of the Caribbean, but was relieved even when that was over.

So he approaches his two parents, separately, about his fear and anxiety.

Parent #1: "Take some Dramamine and 'man up.'" In other words, I assume, be a man. Be more manly. Real men stare down their fears and do it anyway. Parent #1 then makes suggestions for "active imagination" exercises: "Pretend you're an airplane pilot flying a plane," etc.

Parent #2: "Real men don't do anything they don't want to do. Real men don't need to prove their masculinity to anyone." In other words, I assume, be a man. Be more manly. Real men aren't ego-seduced into machismo rites of passage. Parent #2 then makes suggestions for plausible (if untruthful) explanations for how to decline the roller coaster and still save face in front of peers.

They both have a point.

On the one hand, doesn't the boy have a right to define his own masculine identity? And, in a healthy world, shouldn't there be a broad continuum of ways to manifest the masculine archetype? Doesn't a real man give himself that freedom? (Read James Kavanaugh's poetry collection *There Are Men Too Gentle to Live Amongst Wolves*.)

I'm never going to bungy jump. Ever. Why? Because I'm afraid to. You'd have to peel my fingers off the platform and throw me off weeping and pleading. You doubt my masculinity? That says WAY more about you than it does about me, and I don't give a rip anyway. I agree with the comedian Gallagher: "After thirty, it is unwise for your ass ever to be higher than your head."

On the other hand, real men *are* willing to embrace an ever-deepening masculine identity, and that includes facing fears, not allowing fears to conscript joy, duty, accomplishment, or participation in real intimacy. And, oddly enough, braving rituals such as roller coasters, rock climbing, public speaking, fear of cockroaches, getting in a bar fight — well sometimes these things are just what the doctor ordered to help facilitate a symbolic shift in identity and confidence.

When I was six, I was afraid to learn to water ski. My father humiliated me. My mother coddled me. When I was thirty, a bunch of nice kids from the church high school youth group talked me into the lake, attached a ski to my trembling legs, and, on the third try, I was up and flying across the water. A rite of passage. I was delirious with the victory of self. There was now more "man" in me. Without the kids pushing, I never would have done it.

This one's a toughy. What do you think?

I'm left wondering if the boy's dilemma has provoked something in both parents undeveloped and unformed, that maybe neither this mother nor this father has a firm grip on the wholeness of the masculine. The only opinion about which I feel confident is that it's their struggle. Not the boy's.

Maybe they should just tell the boy to trust himself. To stand for the man he most enjoys being.

Sexual courtship is an uneven two-way street

I'm pushing a grocery cart. Whatever is the opposite of "got your mojo going," that's me. More like "got your dull, boring, domestic, middle-class drone going." So I'm surprised by the voice that says, "Do you know anything about peanut butter?"

She's maybe twenty-six. She's holding a different brand of peanut butter in each hand. I tell her I don't work there, but she's not dissuaded: "Which of these is better for you?"

What's wrong with being helpful to your neighbor?

I explain about sugar content, hydrogenated fats, etc. Takes thirty seconds max. I close by pointing to the organic peanut butter. It's by far best for you, but it tends to be an acquired taste for most modern folks.

"Maybe I should come over to your house and try some," she says, head tilted, one eyebrow raised, eyes dancing.

To say I was surprised doesn't begin to describe it. I can't remember the last time somebody flat out "came on" to me. My face turns three sheets of crimson. I mumble something geeky and turn away.

"I'm serious," she says.

I smile and say, "And so is my girlfriend. You wouldn't believe how serious."

Now it's the woman's turn to blush. She begins to apologize profusely. I assuage her embarrassment, tell her not to fret, tell her she had no way of knowing, that I'm not offended. "You made my day," I say with a good-natured wave, "and I hope you find somebody to eat peanut butter with real soon." I push on toward the baking powder.

It's not easy meeting people, and when it comes to love and romance you gotta put yourself out there. I admire the woman.

But what if you replay the entire scene and switch the genders? What if a man says to a woman, "Maybe I should come over to your house and try some?" Why do I think the poor guy would be wearing the peanut butter on his head? Why do I wince imagining a woman's indignant speech about offense and exploitation and I'm not an object and how dare you and men are pigs blah-blah-blah? Why are the rules for sexual attraction and courtship so different for men and women?

I spent the next several weeks asking women whom I respect and admire. And two themes consistently emerged in their answers — one, an objective fact, the other a tragedy.

The objective fact is the imbalance of power. Prison notwithstanding, the average man never spends much time worrying about being raped. When a woman says she's sexually attracted to a man, there is room to celebrate. When a man says he's sexually attracted to a woman, she can't get to the celebration because she's not yet sure she's physically safe. Her hostility to the man's sexuality is the projection of fear.

The tragedy is a pathology in the way we raise women. It is in fact an ancient and terrible lie: If a man is sexually attracted to a woman, then the woman has caused it. That the man is randy for her is now somehow her responsibility. Her sin is being attractive to him *at all*. And her choices are to be the ice princess or the tease. Either way she'll be punished. Her hostility to the man's sexuality is the projection of a twisted shame.

I left the store feeling pleasantly flattered and admiring the woman. I left the store feeling sorry for the next poor guy who tries the same tactic.

And, oh yeah, I know what you're thinking. You're wondering if it occurred to me how long the woman had been standing next to the peanut butter, and whether I was the first guy she'd asked.

Sure, ruin it for me.

Clichés, curiosities abound in online dating world

Time for a journalistic confession: I spent much of July and August lurking about on various online dating services, investigating this accelerating cultural phenomenon. I interviewed scores of men and women.

I have no criticisms of online dating. Really. It's a fine thing. The success stories are real. Some people have met the loves of their lives through an online service, or its progenitor, the now almost vestigial "personal ad." If online dating seems a promising strategy for you, go for it.

But I am still thinking through a list of curiosities I assembled while investigating this particular evolution of cyber-behavior. It seems to me that online dating presupposes a handful of things that might be, well, untrue.

All of these services, for example, advertise their expertise at matching "compatibility." And all of these services presuppose that compatibility rests largely on having a lot in common.

But is it true that great relationships are founded on similarities? It seems to me that profound connections are forged as much or even more by the mystery of differences — how two people create a compelling and passionate union precisely because of the space created by what is *not* the same.

If your lover/mate is too much like you, then one of you is unnecessary. And there isn't a psychological questionnaire on the planet that can measure and predict how and why some differences repel while other differences make us crazy with intrigue and attraction.

I was struck by the number of men and women — especially women — who withheld photos from their profiles. I ended up wondering if these people believed deeply in the myth that looks don't matter, that the Real You is somehow unrelated to the Embodied You, that maybe I'll have a better chance if someone gets to know me through e-mails, IMs, and phone calls. Then my age, my bone structure, my symmetry, my gait, my relative fitness and health, my posture, my physiognomy — all of this will become a happy irrelevance.

It's just not true. What we look like is always a part of dating and courtship. Always.

It became funny to discover how repetitive and similar were the member profiles. Are you considering online dating? Then let me guess: You're tired of the "games." You're not looking for any "players." You're tired of the bar/nightclub "scene." You want to meet someone who will be "honest" with you. You are looking for your "soulmate."

The presupposition I found curious here was the idea that online dating provides a superior way to practice courtship. That meeting someone online was inherently less risky and more honest than meeting someone in a nightclub.

Well, this isn't true either. People misrepresent themselves online at just about the same rate as they do at bars. They lie about their age. They post badly outdated photos. They exaggerate education or income. They disguise their hope to seduce you with the pretense of wanting to get to know you. The relative anonymity of online communication is supposed to provide safety, but I wonder if it just as often invites even more fantasy and fabrication than a bar stool.

Tired of the games? Come on! The game is half the fun. If I want to introduce myself to a woman at a bar, it's likely that I will pop two Altoids in my mouth before heading over. It's a game, however, because I promise you that my breath doesn't always smell like fresh peppermint. I don't always wear this cologne. Some Saturdays, I don't even bathe, for heaven's sake, let alone shave!

"Games" are a normal and natural part of courtship. Online dating seems to think that it can leapfrog The Hunt. That courtship can be reduced to a rational, intentional, and systematic plan. But in the end, we're still just primates, even in cyberspace, dancing our courtship dances, grooming, playing "games," trying to turn the head of a prospective mate.

The idea that we can *decide* to find our soulmate, that we can be intentional about falling in love, well, I just find it a curious idea. Because great love affairs happen. Or they don't. They can't be forged or controlled by logic, structure, or intention. We have the choice, of course, to be open or closed to The Happening, but I'm not convinced we can make The Happening happen.

Online dating provides you the chance to meet your soulmate. True. About the same chance, I think, as going to a bar or nightclub. Or going grocery shopping. Or joining a hiking club. Or volunteering at a youth summer camp.

Or writing a Sunday newspaper column.

What's on the outside matters, too

Have you noticed all the television programs devoted to the topic of cosmetic surgery? Reality shows, medical documentaries, even entire dramatic series are written around doctors whose livelihoods depend on people wanting to rearrange noses, lips, foreheads, ears, wrinkles, breasts, butts, and fat deposits. And it's not just women anymore. Liposuction patients are increasingly men. Cosmetic surgery is an all but mainstream part of middle- and upper-class American life.

It's tempting to look at this phenomenon and wonder if it's nothing more than yet another expression of the ever-increasing materialism, hedonism, and shallowness of American culture. After all, what's on the outside doesn't matter, right? It's what's on the inside that counts. Right?

Ridiculous. What's on the outside is always related to what's on the inside and vice versa. If you've ever known someone who has lost or gained a hundred pounds, then you know this person doesn't merely look different; they are different. If you've ever known an amputee, you know that he is not merely missing a finger or a limb, he is missing part of himself.

If, heaven forbid, I'm ever savagely burned, and you come to the hospital and say, "But the good news, Steven, is that you are still the same person on the inside," then I'm going to ask you to leave. Because I won't be the same person. What happens on the outside changes the inside. What happens on the inside changes the outside. We aren't spirits coincidentally stuffed into people suits. We are embodied human beings.

I listened recently to a woman complain about cosmetic surgery. Vanity. A pathetic capitulation to image and ego. "I'm raising my daughter to value and honor the body she has, not to pine after some image of how the culture thinks a woman ought to look," she says. "What is this culture's fascination with breasts anyway?"

"Probably the same as its fascination with teeth," I reply.

She heard me. She wears braces, and not because of some dental pathology. Nope — she gives her orthodontist a ton of money because she has an investment in how other people think about her *vis* her teeth, because she herself believes deeply that the aesthetics of her teeth say something important to the world about the person she is and the person she wants to be.

To the woman's great credit, she doesn't smack me for observing the teensy-weensy discrepancy between her righteous rampage and her behavior, and she's even willing to listen to my theory about why so many people share this not-always conscious contradiction. It's about sex. Teeth don't connote sexuality the same way that lips and breasts do, so orthodontics don't cause us the same anxiety and ambivalence.

And it's not just about sex; it's about women and sex. We're still not sure we're comfortable with women who consciously and shamelessly reach to claim their sexuality. If it was mostly men we were talking about, this conversation would be different.

So nip and tuck away? That's not my point at all. There are many things disturbing about this new industry. Some patients have motives born of immaturity, psychological wounds, and cultural dereliction that no amount of surgery will ever bring to wholeness.

No — I'm saying there are also perfectly fine and rational and even laudable reasons to seek cosmetic surgery. The desire to consciously claim a powerful and joyful sexual identity can be such a reason.

What is it about sexuality, especially a woman's sexuality, that is so unsettling to us?

Reconsider the true meaning of narcissism

Narcissism is not what it appears to be.

It appears to be a falling in love with oneself. An inflated sense of self. A great hubris. A thinking too highly of oneself. Thinking others are inferior. Cocky. Condescending. Arrogant.

Nothing could be further from the truth. Narcissism is the precise opposite of love for oneself. It is in fact a tragedy of self-loathing.

Narcissus is not punished by the gods because he falls in love with himself. No; he is punished because he looks into a pool of water and falls in love with his *image*. He doesn't lean over the water and say, "Wow, now that's a beautiful man!" He leans over and says, "Wow, that is one compelling reflection!"

Why would someone fall in love with his image? Because the reality of self is broken and wounded. Painful and unbearable. Even terrifying. Blind infatuation with one's image is a strategy not of self-love but of self-hatred. It is an escape. A committed narcissist defends those images at all cost because his ultimate commitment is to avoid seeing and knowing himself.

Attempt to look behind the images and you will suffer the narcissist's rage. He will control, demean, belittle, withhold, and withdraw. Turn passive-aggressive. The aggrandizements will actually escalate. If necessary, the narcissist will attempt to ruin you.

In the case of pathological narcissism (thankfully rare), the narcissist might try to destroy you, or talk you into destroying yourself. Ask the surviving relatives of The Family, headed by Charles Manson (California, 1969). Ask the surviving relatives of The People's Temple, headed by the Rev. Jim Jones (Guyana, 1978.) Folks with an insufficient sense of self are vulnerable to guys like this. If God says drink the Kool-Aid and die, I'd better drink the Kool-Aid.

Groupies help a narcissist keep the image polished and running. Groupies need this guy's image as much as he does.

But, more commonly, the trump card of the ordinary narcissist is walking away. Your punishment for daring to inquire about the person behind the image is that you will be abandoned.

Notice the exclusive use of masculine pronouns. I'm not a sexist; it's deliberate. In our current culture, an overwhelming disproportion of narcissism is represented in men. There are observable dynamics in Western Civilization that virtually guarantee most modern males will spend their lives struggling with narcissistic features in their personality. (Or not struggling, if they're too narcissistic to care.)

I've stashed a title for the book I want to write about narcissism. It will be called *I Dare You, How Dare You.* That's the game, see. The narcissist will slowly escalate behaviors of control and entitlement to see if you'll notice. He'll be selfish. Oblivious. Demanding. He'll sulk and withdraw if he doesn't get his way. His behavior presupposes his knowledge of the way things ought to be.

This part of the game is called "I dare you." Meaning, I dare you to set a boundary with me. In fact, I won't respect you if you continue to let me treat you this way. Go on. I double-dog dare you to call my behavior into question.

So, if you respect yourself at all, you call the narcissist to account.

Now comes part two: How dare you! The narcissist denies, flares up, defends, ranting incredulity. You hurt his feelings. You've misunderstood him.

If you capitulate under the assault of "how dare you," he'll lose respect for you. If you confront him, he'll withdraw in a huff because you're so critical and nobody really understands him.

Good luck, girls.

I often marvel that you women fall in love with us guys at all. I think it's a miracle that so many of you keep coming home and wanting to stay with us.

My guess is you know us better than we could imagine. Maybe we'd be frightened to consider that the jig is up, that you already know we're full of horse patootie.

Maybe we can't comprehend the part of your love that is compassion for our frailty. Maybe you saw long ago that "arrogant bastard" is a cheap disguise.

Maybe, on some intuitive level, women just know what us poor schlub guys ought to know about ourselves — that before this boorish behavior was draining the patience of this nice woman, it was an attempt to survive a terrible psychic injury and its aftermath: insecurity, self-doubt, and self-hatred.

The fix for narcissism is to love oneself *more*.

Anger and violence are disguises for grief and loss

He's a house. A mansion, actually. Body builder. His arms are as big as my legs, and more powerful. In the past, he made his living as a bouncer. Today, he sweats in the Mojave Desert sun in the seats of backhoes and other large construction equipment. I don't know if this man eats quiche, but I doubt it, and either way I'm not about to ask him.

So, when he tells me the story of the chuckwalla, I'm surprised by his emotion.

Not that he *shows* any emotion, mind you. But you can see the added tension in his jaw. The way his breathing changes. The curtain that falls over his eyes. A guy like this grieves in a place so deep inside himself that it becomes like light from the sun. The distance between its source and his experience of it is a long, long way.

He's working the backhoe. He glances to his left, and there on a rock sits the chuckwalla. The reptile watches the man and the machine, motionless. The man feels a connection to the chuckwalla. He greets the big lizard. Speaks to him. Then tosses a handful of sunflower seeds toward him.

The creature moves down from the rock and begins to feast upon the gift from the man. The man has a new friend.

Now the lizard scoots behind the backhoe and around, watching from the man's right. More sunflower seeds. More conversation. Work always goes easier and faster with a friend.

There is movement in the man's peripheral vision. A co-worker suddenly looms over the chuckwalla, brandishing a shovel aloft. And just like that, the chuckwalla is dead. Crushed in one stupid, cruel moment.

Why does the co-worker kill the lizard? Because he can.

The man with the shovel — boy, really — has no idea what peril he is in. The lizard's friend has gone mercenary. He has, in the past, hurt people for less reason than this. He is detached, coolly and quietly contemplating what he'll do after he loses his job because he has assaulted a co-worker. Perhaps he'll be leaving this construction site in handcuffs even as the chuckwalla's murderer leaves in an ambulance.

All his life it's been like this. Anger, intimidation, violence — these things have been the beginning and the end of his repertoire for managing life since he can remember.

So what the man does next is remarkable. He calls a woman. Instead of dishing out pain to the world, he talks about his own pain with his girlfriend. To say this doesn't come naturally to the man is like saying eating alfalfa doesn't come naturally to a shark.

His father died more than 35 years ago, before the man's fifth birthday. Memories are scant, but the man remembers his father caught and raised chuckwallas — delighted in the little creatures. Loved them. Pampered them. The boy remembers helping his father care for magnificent reptiles.

This is not just any lizard. It's a family totem, an animal that carries for the man a memory, a legacy, a part of his identity. The connection is spiritual. And deep.

The kid with the shovel was not just stupid and cruel to an innocent beast; he assaulted the man's father, the man's family, his memories, and most especially a place inside the man where tenderness and nurture still live. Of course his grief is profound.

Behind every movement of anger and violence is something that we have lost, and the grief that comes as a companion to that loss. When we have the courage to embrace our grief, then anger and violence become less necessary.

In the past, the man would have honored his father with a silly boy's broken jaw and a jail sentence. Today, he honors his father with his grief.

Vitality and self-respect are sexually attractive

In 2006, a reader wrote me an honest and poignant letter about his wife's weight gain, and his struggle to maintain an erotic connection with her. This prompted a five-week series of columns, and the most delicious flurry of reader mail. I've adapted the series for the book into one long article.

A reader writes: **"My wife is fat. I've been married twenty-one years, and if I showed you our wedding pictures, you wouldn't know it's the same woman. I'm not talking a few pounds. It's got to be more like fifty. I'm just not attracted to her anymore. She knows it, and I know it hurts her. She says she's the same person on the inside, and wishes I could just see past it. Can a guy learn to see past it?"**

I'll answer this, good man, but you should know I'm gonna get grouchy mail.

On the one hand, the cosmetic expectations of our culture — particularly (but not exclusively) for women — are unrealistic, cruel, and, frankly, shallow. Do you remember the myth of Pygmalian? In our culture, we carve a fixed and narrow image of "desirable woman," and worship it, leaving the vast majority of women straining, obsessing, starving themselves, even mutilating themselves hoping to inch closer to the image they will never attain. The net result is that we teach women to despise themselves as a way of life.

When it comes to psychosexual development, sometimes I think Hugh Hefner practically raised me. Him and Victoria's Secret catalogues. *Sports Illustrated* Swimsuit Issues. From as early as I can remember, this world hammered into my brainstem the prototype for "desirable woman." This, this, this, this — flashing like a neon sign in front of a diner. It was less an education, and more of a trained behavioral response, like teaching a rat to press the lever for cocaine in a college psych experiment.

And Hefner's vision mutates! His first *Playboy* centerfold, Marilyn Monroe, circa 1954, would never today be invited for a test shoot, let alone be chosen as a Playmate. By today's measure, Marilyn would be overweight. Chunky. A buxom lass. The women who hang with Hef today all come from the same cookie cutter. Short. Petite. Maybe 105 pounds. Collagen lips. Inflated breasts. Straight, platinum blond hair.

There's more diversity in the hamster cage at Petco.

On the other hand . . .

Obesity in America is a flat-out health crisis. Pandemic. America is fat. We eat compulsively and badly. Our collective relationship with food is every bit the acculturated immaturity as are our ideas about who is sexually desirable.

You might convince me that my standards for aesthetic preference (what people look like) are cultural whimsy. But you will never similarly convince me regarding the deeper issues of fitness and vitality. Vitality is attractive. Sexy. It is Life Force.

Obesity must ultimately cost us some measure of vitality. Fat embalms us. And that *is* a fair subject for objective, critical inquiry.

And lastly . . .

Significant weight gain is virtually never a benign coincidence. It means something. Sometimes, in some cultures, it means prosperity and happiness.

But more often, when people struggling with chronic weight issues seek therapy, they find those issues connected with issues such as self-respect, depression, sexuality. Sometimes weight gain is self-loathing. Others use it as an armor against intimacy. Still others use it as a way to manage childhood issues or to tell their spouse to go to hell.

If the essential message from one spouse to another is "I no longer care about my own health, vitality, and wholeness, but I insist you still desire me," then, ouch, how can that not feel like rejection? Like being discarded. It's not easy to respect someone who doesn't respect themselves, let alone desire them.

The same person on the inside? No way. What happens to our bodies happens to our soul. What happens in our soul ultimately will be expressed in our bodies. This is Cosmic Law.

Imagine an alcoholic spouse saying, "Just look past all the hooch I'm slamming down, because I'm still the same person you married on the inside." Oh really? Last time I looked, marriage vows called us to love and honor our spouse, not participate in his/her denial and self-destruction.

Can you learn to see past your wife's weight gain, to eroticize intimacy, and find a new and deeper way to desire her? Maybe. Probably. Does the average American male need to do some serious growing up about this? Absolutely.

But a different question is, can you learn to see past what the weight gain means? Depends on what it means. Maybe not. And maybe you shouldn't. Maybe it would be like lying to the kids to cover for an alcoholic.

I'm saying that what your wife is asking you might not be altogether in her own best interest.

A reader writes: **"Recently, I read your response to the man with the fat wife. What intrigued me was your assertion that this man could probably learn to see past his wife's weight and be able to** regain intimacy with her. Now, I could understand maintaining my love for her but intimacy? How does one achieve this? Can you possibly recommend some reading material regarding this matter?"

I received a lot of letters like this. Most men DON'T take their marriage vows lightly, despite the common cultural prejudice that men are shallow about matters of love, sex, and romance.

My contention is (and remains) that if our spouse (husband or wife) is engaged in a behavior grounded in the loss of self-respect, the loss of willingness to engage life with vitality and intention, a behavior indicative of deeper crisis, a behavior indicative of deliberately distancing the marriage, or worse, an obviously self-destructive behavior, then "learning to see past" the behavior is inappropriate. It is an invitation to participate in the pathology, as we say in my field.

The answer to that invitation is always, "No, thank you." We don't abandon our spouse and the marriage. We confront the behavior. We say "This behavior is not okay."

The same response would be required, frankly, if our spouse became bulimic or anorexic. Those behaviors aren't okay either.

Obesity is a medical problem, and, in most cases, a problem connected to psycho-emotional malaise like those described above.

Next, let me say that I simply reject the idea that, if it is true love, then looks don't matter. Equally absurd is the reflexive prejudice about men: If a man no longer feels erotically attracted to his wife because she has gained fifty pounds, that man must be shallow.

Ridiculous.

Male sexuality is more neurologically wired optically — provoked (at least initially) by what he sees. Female sexuality includes the biological drive to "be seen." If you're interested in such things, recent research observes these same behaviors in our closest genetic cousins, chimpanzees. We can insist a man hate himself for this (isn't that sexist?), but it isn't going to change. It's just a fact.

Yet, two other things are also true:

For a man, the bonds of love and sexuality are not *only* made up of what he sees. For a healthy man, it never would be enough. I have more than once been initially attracted to a woman I thought (and still think) is drop-dead, take-your-breath-away beautiful, sexy, etc., only to find myself perplexed a few minutes or a few days later by how paradoxically "unattracted" I was to her. Something else was missing, even if I could never quite put it into concrete terms.

What a man decides looks erotically desirable is only partly innate. Back to the chimp research, for example. The first females to mate with the strongest males have the more symmetrical faces. The most desirable females are fit and healthy.

But for human males, the much larger part of what we "like" to look at is programmed, as it were, by culture. Middle Eastern men, for example, regularly describe our supermodels as "underfed" and "scrawny." A reader letter alerted me last week to a PBS special about a Slavic culture where men desire very large women. These men insist women risk their health in obesity the same way many American men insist women risk their health with high-risk dieting and cosmetic surgery. I maintain what I said last Tuesday: Modern American men have been programmed with an image of desirability that ranges from cruelly unrealistic to pure fiction.

But the good news is, if a man's erotic attractions are more programmed than innate, then we DO have some real capacity to be reprogrammed, to re-wire how we make bonds with women that generate authentic sexual desire.

Let's put to bed our previous discussion of obesity as both a medical crisis and as indicative of wider psycho-emotional crisis. Let's say we're talking about the more common phenomenon of changes brought by age, child bearing, metabolic shifts, genetic body type, or, regrettably, disfiguring tragedies (burns, amputations, etc.). In my answer, I'm going to focus primarily on men reconnecting with women, though obviously women, too, have their own erotic preferences that can be challenged by all these issues.

Men might do well to first sit down and have a talk with themselves . . . a "come to Jesus" sort of meeting recognizing that we have been sold a bill of goods. The women we been taught to be attracted to largely don't exist. We're hot for digital illusions, airbrushes, and cosmetic interpretations of women instead of real flesh. If it helps you to mobilize some old-fashioned ego indignation, well, remind yourself that a fair number of strippers think men are stupid, a fact that we're all too ready to confirm about $300 later.

Next, we might do well to take a crash course in women and their bodies. Pregnancy is a wide variable. It ravages some women's bodies more than others, scarring abdominal skin, permanently shifting the shape of hips, breasts, even feet. For some women, no amount of sit-ups can entirely eradicate the signature sag of a post-maternal belly. There is, too, a genetic given-ness to metabolic rates and the changes in those rates as women age.

We don't change our erotic preferences by chanting "I'm a shallow man-toad, I'm a shallow man-toad." In fact, we don't "look past" changes we don't prefer. What we do is reconsider our ideas of what the changes mean.

This actually happens spontaneously for many husbands during pregnancy. It's a not-often-published fact that, during pregnancy, many husbands find their erotic attraction for their mate intensifies. This is because the weight gain and the changes in body don't convey negative meanings but positive ones. Her growing belly and swollen breasts mean celebration for the husband. He attaches to it with happiness and, frankly, a kind of "normal narcissism" that generates real desire and the yen to connect in sexual courtship. With a little logistic care, couples can enjoy this courtship through the seventh or eighth month of an uncomplicated pregnancy.

After the baby is born, a man can attach the meanings of gratitude, celebration, even heroism to the "sacrifice" of his wife's body in service to creation. These sorts of changes aren't about a loss of vitality or self-respect. Just the opposite. They are the natural consequences of PARTICIPATING in an ultimate vitality: baby-making!

Here's another example, this time from the woman's side of the fence.

I once knew a woman who had fallen in love with a blind man. Her presenting issue was her sense of confusion about sexual courtship. The deeper issue was her sense of grief. Grief? Yep. Loving this man meant letting go of ways of being a woman that were deeply meaningful to her. Satisfying and enjoyable. To wit: primping and pampering. Dressing sexy. Colors, textures, and design lines. Accessories. Hair styles. Make-up. Lingerie.

Here's what I *didn't* do: "Things will get better, ma'am, when you realize what a shallow, vain woman you are . . . when you realize that the only thing that matters is who you are on the inside." (Gentlemen, if your significant other comes down the stairs dressed hot and says, "How do I look?" I would advise against saying, "Honey, it doesn't matter how you look because I only care about the real you on the inside.")

Here's what I *did* do: I affirmed her new love by affirming her loss. The loss was real. She's not shallow or vain. She's a normal, healthy woman. Acknowledging loss is the first step toward resolving it. If she was to value the new relationship, her task was to learn a new and very different language of courtship and enticement. And she didn't then start wearing sweatshirts all the time. She continued to choose great style and grooming because she liked the way it made her feel about herself.

In 1980, I saw the film *The Elephant Man.* It was the story of John Merrick, born in England in 1862. Merrick suffered from Proteus Syndrome, an extremely rare disease that causes abnormal, unchecked growth of bones and skin. The make-up for John Hurt (the actor who played Merrick) was painstakingly crafted using photographs and Merrick's intact skeleton on display at the English Hospital museum where Merrick lived his last days.

The film makes you wait a good while before you see Merrick. And when I did finally see him, I had to confront a powerful physical reaction. My gorge rose. I was nauseated. Had a parasympathetic reaction. My breathing changed. John Merrick was hideous beyond words. (Ask yourself right now if this makes me "shallow.")

About an hour later, I was watching a scene wherein Merrick is reciting Shakespeare with a local English stage actress. The Inner Voice tapped me on the shoulder and said, "Psst . . . don't mean to interrupt, but have you noticed that you are no longer noticing that John Merrick is hideous?"

Oh my. It was true. I'd met John. Somehow, when I wasn't looking, I'd gotten connected to the character of John Merrick. Make no mistake, Merrick looked the same, and the way he looked was terrible indeed. But somehow Merrick's "looks" no longer carried the same meaning. His terrifying deformities no longer terrified.

My experience of this film taught me I was responsible not only for what I looked at, but what I thought and believed about what I looked at. What happened in the film was preconscious; but I knew, then, that I must have the power to make it conscious.

The definition of shallow is NOT, then, someone who enjoys being fit, healthy, and attractive, or someone who enjoys looking at fitness, health, and beauty. A shallow person is someone who refuses to take responsibility for what they think and believe about what they see. A shallow person spends his/her life thinking it's the mate's responsibility to "turn me on," all the while refusing to realize it's largely me who decides when and with whom to have desire based on what I think and believe.

And that is my answer to your question. If we can get connected (or re-connected) to our spouse, this often changes what physical appearance *means.*

If, as men, we can throw off the absurdity of a psycho-sexual acculturation, leaving us chasing images of women both unrealistic and even fictional, if we have no grounds to think our wife's weight gain qualifies as a serious health problem, if there is no evidence our wife's weight gain reflects the negative meaning of willful loss of vitality, giving up on the marriage, fear of sex, depression, or similarly unacceptable conditions of heart, soul, and mind (which, in my opinion, should never be "looked past") . . .

. . . if, on the other hand, what we are looking at is the more or less normal shifts of metabolism and aging, the changes wrought by pregnancy, the extra pounds that appear during a time of bereavement or perhaps a time of extreme pressure and focus (graduate school, caregiving for an ailing relative, intense career pressure, etc.). . . .

. . . or, if what we are looking at is the consequences of illness — thyroid disorder, steroid intervention, amputation, surgical scars, injuries precluding the possibility of regular exercise. . . .

. . . then we don't confront our spouse. We confront ourselves.

It has been fascinating kicking around the idea of "shallow" with my readers. I'm convinced we often use this accusation as a defense, rather than as an accurate description of someone. For example, I often help people (more often women) construct the "List of Non-Negotiables" after a disappointing break-up. The List helps her defend herself against betraying herself and repeating past mistakes: "Has to have a college degree . . . Must have a job . . . Can't be an addict. . . ." Does this list make her shallow? (Gee, ma'am, there are lots of great guys out there with only a GED!)

Would you think someone shallow who concludes they don't/can't make erotic connections to certain racial groups? How about a man who says, "I'm just not attracted to tiny, petite women"? Heck, I have a friend who only wants to date Republicans! Now *that's* shallow! (Okay, I'm just mad because she won't have dinner with me.)

Why does attention to weight bring the accusation of "shallow," but not education levels or job status? It's a defense, that's why.

The legitimate criticism of "shallow" has to do with the inability or unwillingness to see past what we like to look at to the deeper wholeness of a human being. But we abuse the idea of shallow applying it to someone just because they have an aesthetic preference for Y instead of Z.

Next, I was flat out moved by the number of folks (men!) who wrote to express real sorrow about no longer being physically attracted to overweight mates, yet still loving them deeply and desiring to "reconnect." These people weren't shallow, but neither did they give in to the silliness of "looks don't matter." It was an honor to hear these stories of committed love.

I was surprised by the number of women who wrote to say, "Yeah, what about women with overweight husbands?" Actually, if you reverse the genders, you get more similarities than differences. Women are not wired as visually as men, neuro-sexually speaking, and they aren't acculturated with the same unrealistic and cruelly narrow standards for what constitutes "good looking." But women do have eyes, and they enjoy using them. Women can be and are often just as disappointed (and unattracted) when a husband gives up on fitness and vitality (read: gets fat) as when a wife gives up.

True love requires confrontation as often as it requires acceptance. It is inappropriate to "look past" self-destructive behavior. Great marriages are made of spouses who, when appropriate, say to their mates, "Behavior X is *not* okay. It constitutes shoddy marital practice and equivocal marital commitment. No, I won't look past it. I won't tolerate it. Fix it."

And lastly, I greatly admire the women who wrote such intelligent and moving letters simultaneously accepting men as men yet wrapping the sorority in encouragement and advocacy against a culture whose messages to women are so toxic.

"When a woman stops looking into the mirror that is a man's face, things get better. She needs her own mirror. She needs to delight in being beautiful in herself. For herself. Then the men will come. I guarantee it." —S.P., Evergreen, Colorado.

"People have forgotten (or been misled) from witnessing the wholeness of beauty, which includes heart, confidence, and truth. The synergy of such a combination is a substance that cannot be identified. It simply 'is' for all its glory. It causes us to cherish and grow old with someone whose outer beauty was intended to be fleeting." —G.C., Houston, Texas.

"And I just thought of another thing that never fails to tick me off. When I go in for my annual gyno appointment, I am accosted with pictures, ads, brochures, pamphlets, etc., offering me ways to improve or redefine my body. I find it irritating and even unethical to visit a physician's office and be subjected to this crap. I don't know where this is all heading. I guess the bright side for you is that you'll have even more therapy clients." — A.P., Greenville, South Carolina.

"Have you read *Beauty Junkies: Inside Our $15 Billion Obsession with Cosmetic Surgery*, by Alex Kuczynski? Get this quote:

'Admitting you've had the latest wrinkle filler is no longer a mark of shame; on the contrary, it is a status symbol in the mind of the twenty-first century consumer who believes that self-maintenance is a deeply moral obligation.'" — L.M., Tempe, Arizona.

My readers rock.

Grief and Loss Matters

EVERY HELLO BEGINS A GOODBYE. Every well-said goodbye makes possible a new hello. Life is about saying goodbye . . . and hello. And goodbye. And hello. And so it goes until the day comes when we say goodbye to this life and hello to the mystery over yonder.

So many goodbyes — the experience of loss is in the very fabric of this existence, and it's more than just the relentless presence of random tragedies, accidents, disease, and death. Moments begin and end. Relationships die. Possibilities die. Dreams die. Times and places come and go. To welcome one thing inevitably requires bidding one or more other things farewell.

Saying hello to finger foods for your baby means saying goodbye to the days of tenderness and intimacy at the breast. Choosing a career in medicine means not choosing a career in farming. Saying an exclusive yes to one lover means saying no to other potential lovers. Yep. Commitment is a grief issue.

If we are to become human beings, our ego must die. And it's usually not pretty. The ego dies a dog's death. We must say goodbye to self-importance.

When we are wounded by loss, what we bleed is grief. We have lost something or someone or some time or some place and now something about us must die, too. It is hard work, this grief. It requires uncommon courage to do it well.

Grief has many names. Nostalgia is a grieving over a lost-yet-remembered innocence. Despair is the name of the grief we feel when we have lost hope. Longing is grieving a future not yet here. Cynicism is the grief of no longer being able to risk belief in essential goodness. Guilt is the grief we feel when we abandon our values.

Grief has many expressions. Some cultures teach and value dramatic, emotional expression. Other cultures teach and value the restraint of emotion, and replace it with narrative and storytelling. Some cultures have elaborate ceremonies, rituals, and assigned symbols. Still other cultures — mine, for example — teach and value intellectualizing and denying grief. "Getting over it" is the American Way.

To grieve honestly and well, we give up some control. We sit quietly with our sadness. We stop arguing with the facts. We breathe our sadness in. We breathe it out. And sometimes our grief just has a mind of its own. That flat, empty feeling. Quiet stoicism. Lump in the throat. Weeping. Crying. Wailing, shoulders shaking and breath coming in gulps.

Sometimes grief takes you by the arm and drags you unwilling to a place primitive and primordial. It's beyond reason. You go a little bit crazy. Your legs fail you. Your nose runs. You forget to swallow your own saliva. You make terrible noises. You lay on the floor and moan, bellow, and thrash. The grief possesses your body, rolls you up into a fetal position, then sends you sprawling onto your back. You pound the carpet. You hold your guts in both hands.

It's a kind of dying. Terrifying, but holy. And if we are to be faithful on the faithful human journey, sometimes necessary. Sometimes the only way we can be whole.

Unacknowledged grief turns to poison and malice. Couples that can't grieve often divorce. People who can't grieve sometimes kill — themselves or others.

A police officer once described to me the practice of an inner-city gang wherein gang members would tattoo a tear drop on their face to represent every person they had murdered. The irony was compelling. The young gangbanger cannot cry, so he paints his tears on his face. And for every tear that he cannot cry, someone has to die.

In 1995 I left my job as a counselor and took a job as director of bereavement services in a large hospice. "Oooh, don't you think that's going to be a real downer," my friend says, "dealing with grief all the time?"

"It's always about grief," I say to my friend. "No one comes to therapy who hasn't lost something."

It's true. It's sad to have incompetent or cruel parents. It's sad to waste your life and ruin relationships with addiction. Divorce is sad. It's sad to love a teenager who holds you in contempt. It's sad to live in fear. To despise oneself. To never know oneself. To lose oneself.

To live well, we must learn how to say goodbye well, and often. Well-said goodbyes are conscious and intentional. We give thanks for what was good. We acknowledge and, if appropriate, account for what was bad. We forgive what we can forgive, and allow our goodbye to separate us from the rest.

Healthy goodbyes acknowledge loss. Broken hearts don't kill us. Quite the contrary, it is precisely the denial of our broken heart that can become destructive and even lethal.

We don't heal grief by gritting our teeth. We don't heal grief by distracting ourselves with drinking, drugging, and other "acting out" behavior. We don't merely let time pass, because it's not true that time heals wounds. We don't heal grief with rationalities or bumper stickers or platitudes or optimism or cheap religion.

The only way to heal grief is to grieve.

To love anything is to decide to become vulnerable to loss. Check that — to love anything *guarantees* the experience of loss. The only alternative is to decide not to love . . . which, of course, is the worst kind of loss.

To understand ambiguity takes clarity of vision

Nobody knows why things work out the way they do.

I admired my wife's skirt from across the room twice and we had two babies. Life was good. Then we had three miscarriages in sixteen months. Life was not good. We turned our grief on each other and fought. I had the impression she thought I should fix the problem the way you fix a busted vacuum cleaner. She had the impression she had failed me. We understood why the characters in the Hebrew Bible so often saw fertility and children as a sign of God's favor, and why they saw barren wombs as a sign of God's abandonment or displeasure. And the doctors? They insisted "these things just happen."

These things just happen? You charge us thousands of dollars and then have the nerve to tell us these things just happen? Yep. Three doctors gave us the same diagnosis: ambiguity.

We hate ambiguity. Really hate it. We prefer a universe we can control and manage. Tit for tat. If this, then that. If we live upright, moral lives, good things will happen. If we're scoundrels, bad things will happen. There's a plan. The plan might be a mystery to us, but we assure ourselves that beyond the mystery there is a plan. Which is to say there is ultimately no mystery at all. Our response to ambiguity is to deny its possibility.

Popular religion is a common strategy in our efforts to trump ambiguity. We embrace elaborate religious schemes to make ambiguity less ambiguous. Karma, God, free will — some comprehensible force in the universe decides who gets cancer, who wins a slot machine jackpot, which islands get clobbered by tsunamis, whose children get rescued and whose children inhale a lung-full of Indian Ocean. Those who celebrate are considered blessed, protected, chosen. Those who suffer are being tested or being punished or "it's a mystery but not really because there's a plan." As horrible as it feels to think we might *deserve* to have our son or daughter die . . . well, we actually prefer that feeling over the alternative of ambiguity.

We hate ambiguity because it does not provide ready-made meaning, and without meaning our lives quickly become unbearable. This is not to say that ambiguity cannot yield meaning, only to say that ambiguity can never be neutralized by cheap and easy meaning-making schemes. To find meaning in ambiguity — especially in the ambiguity of suffering — we must be willing to suffer ambiguity, to let ambiguity be what it is. Nobody knows why things happen. Nobody knows why things work out the way they do.

To find meaning in ambiguity, we must do the work of humility. Humility relates us rightly and properly to the universe. We don't decide when and where tsunamis strike. Sometimes our every care and precaution does not avert tragedy. Stuff happens. That's all we know for certain.

Humility is not so bad. Humility makes gratitude possible. For example, as I type this, my third son, Joseph, now three years old, is in and out of my lap, patting me with his little hands and laying his head against my chest. His hair smells good. He wants to know if I'll play dinosaurs with him. And what I am is grateful — not entitled, not deserved, not enlightened, and certainly not in charge of much. I'm grateful precisely because I have no idea why Joseph is here, or how he got here, or why I get to be his father. I'm grateful precisely because Joseph doesn't *have* to be here, and might not be here tomorrow. It's a blessed ambiguity.

Sorry to write and run, but I've got to go play dinosaurs.

There's no reason to apologize for tears

The woman in this story is real fiction — a composite character of men and women I've met hundreds of times in therapy. It is pure coincidence if you recognize yourself in this story. Or pure synchronicity, depending on the way you like looking at the world.

⚜

The woman is trying to tell me her story. But she stops in midsentence and sets her jaw. There's a slight tremor of the head and shoulders. A brief, miniature earthquake. She puts down an internal mutiny, and proceeds with her account.

She talks a little faster now, as if she will beat her emotions to some finish line in an intra-psychic race. I suddenly think of Jack and the Beanstalk, remembering how Jack tiptoed quietly past the sleeping giant in hopes of stealing the giant's treasures without waking his wrath. This woman is trying to steal her story over to me without waking her giant emotions.

But the giant rests uneasily. Her throat cuts her off as neatly as if someone had tightened a rope around her neck. She takes a deep breath and holds it. She waits. I wait. She exhales, and goes on talking. So far so good.

But now her voice trails off, like someone pulled a plug. Like someone ran out of gas. Like the sigh of a steam iron. Her jaw and mouth tremble. Her eyes go big and round, and not with surprise. No. It turns out you can hold more water in your eyes if you make them big and round and tip your head slightly back. There's a rule, see, that you're not really crying if nothing has actually fallen out of your eyes.

Now she pretends something is in her eye. Now she reaches for a tissue and pretends to mend her mascara. She covers her index finger with the tissue and runs it under her left eye, across the bridge of her nose, and under her right eye. And back again. Over and over. I think of windshield wipers. *Whish-click, whish-click, whish-click . . . .*

It's here that, back before I knew what I was doing, I might have put on my Empathic Face and said, "It's okay to cry." But a skillful supervisor once responded to this therapeutic technique by saying to me, "What's that about? Are you the Crying Authorization Board?" He asked me to examine the implicit arrogance of letting people give you money in hopes you might grant your benevolent permission for them to cry. "Isn't it more important that people come to terms with their own values about their own tears?" he said.

Needless to say, I no longer give people permission to cry. Or take it away. Talk to me while you cry or talk to me while you don't cry. Or are pretending not to cry. You won't see a huge change in how I'm there with you.

The funny thing about tears is they don't necessarily mean this, that, or the other. Their presence does not guarantee a healthy grief. Their absence is not evidence of the denial of grief. I've known people who, on average, need to think less and cry more. I've known people who, on average, need to think more and give in to their tears less. I have real empathy, mind you, for real human vulnerability. But, surprisingly enough, some people are habituated to use high emotion to *avoid* vulnerability. I've learned not to have any particular response to tears just because someone is crying.

Here's an astonishing metaphor: I think of crying a lot like I think of a full bladder. When you gotta go, you gotta go. People largely trust themselves to know when they need a restroom. They don't need or seek my permission. They just go.

I think of tears that way. So just go.

The woman begins to weep. She covers her face with her hands. Shame. She holds her hands up in the posture of apology and surrender and chokes out the words "I'm sorry" through her teeth.

"For what?" I asked sincerely. She points at her face, as if her countenance is sufficient evidence for her offense to me. And with all kindness I say, "I make it a general rule never to accept apologies from people who haven't injured me. Did you do something wrong to me about which I'm unaware?"

"I promised myself I wouldn't cry," she says.

"Oh, then your apology is misplaced," I say. "You owe yourself an apology. You broke your own rules."

"Why should it be against the rules to cry?" she demands.

"I don't know, ma'am. It's your rule."

Grieving parents need to show kids optimistic side

It was nice of this woman to trust me with her story, and to give me permission to tell it.

The woman picks up her eighth-grade daughter from school and is driving home. Thirty-nine years old. Single parent.

The woman feels a familiar melancholy as her daughter gushes about receiving an award in photography class. Sure, she's happy for her first-born. But there's no one to tell, no partner with whom to share the Proud Parent Moment. In a cruel irony, the girl's joy provokes the mother's loneliness. The woman has been divorced for fourteen months.

It wasn't her choice.

Her cell phone rings. A friend and colleague. "Hey, I have Toby here with me in the car," the woman says. "Why don't I call you back when I get home."

"Was that Dad?" the girl asks.

"Nope," the woman answers.

The air seems to thicken around the little girl. The woman puts her intuitive flash into words: "Toby, do you think that was my boyfriend?"

The girl whips her head around in wide-eyed surprise. "How did you know that?" the girl asks.

"It wasn't my boyfriend, sweetie. I don't *have* a boyfriend." The girl turns her gaze away with a soft nod. Silence caves in, and Mom drives on.

"Daddy really broke your heart, didn't he?"

The question catches the woman off guard. She doesn't have time to find her Politically Correct Everything Is Fine Divorced Parent Persona. She doesn't take her eyes off the road. "There are no words to describe it," she says.

"You're never going to understand it, are you?"

(What has gotten into her? My daughter is channeling some wise old woman.)

"No, honey, I'm never going to understand it," the woman says.

(Maybe I should turn on the radio.)

"It would have been easier if he had died in a car accident, wouldn't it?"

Now Mom pulls the car to the side of the road. She turns to face her daughter. "Honey, that's terrible! I don't want your dad to die in a car accident!"

"I didn't say that, Mom. I said you'd at least understand that way."

Mom contemplates the Wise Woman disguised as her thirteen-year-old.

"Honey, are you worried about me?"

The Wise Woman dissolves back into a little girl. Her countenance falls and tears come. "Yeeesssss," she wails, "I'm afraid you're never gonna be happy again!"

The woman has been grieving. She has felt bad for a long time, but this is the very first time she has felt *bad* about feeling bad.

"I will be happy again, I promise," the woman says to her daughter. "I'll find a way to be happy if I have to rewire what happiness *means*."

"It sure would be a lot more fun," the girl says hopefully.

❧❦❧

My therapeutic specialty is grief. And my overriding prejudice is that the only way to heal grief is to grieve, that the fastest way out of grief is into it and through it.

But the woman's story spins my head around. Turns out there are some bereavements we cannot afford to indulge. Our children are watching. They need to see us believe in life. Love life. They are learning from us what to *do* with tragedy and loss.

I'm not saying deny your losses. I'm not saying fake it when your kids are around. They'll see through that in a heartbeat. Of course it's okay for your children to see you cry.

But moms and dads can't afford to give up. Cash it in. Go through the motions. Because, despite what it might seem — despite the normal, clamoring neediness and narcissism of kids — children carry in their hearts a desperate wish for their parents' happiness.

Children learn life is good primarily by watching their parents love it.

Amish teach valuable lessons about fear

Who knows exactly when Charles Carl Roberts IV stopped being merely troubled and gave himself entirely over to evil? But evil it was that led him down the dirt drive and past the white pastoral fence into a one-room Amish schoolhouse to kill children. When law enforcement intervened, he killed himself, falling with all irony under a sign reading "Visitors Welcome."

Now the driveway is barricaded. Signs say "No trespassing." Geraldo Rivera suggests we arm — with guns — young school boys to protect girls from future perpetrators. Can't decide if that's the worst idea I've ever heard or the most tasteless parody.

I'm not Amish, and I don't want to be. But that doesn't mean I think my way of life is in any way superior. Actually, horses and buggies and milking cows starts to look pretty good when you're wishing you were dead well into your second hour of waiting at the Department of Motor Vehicles, or when you're breathing smoke and shouting conversation at your date over nightclub music that vibrates your bone marrow and loosens the fillings in your teeth. (God I'm old!)

What I respect about the Amish — what inspires me — is their particular witness of peace and innocence wrought through radical simplicity and the grace of hard work. Their way of life is transparent. Vulnerable. Measured by the agreed-upon madness of my world, the Amish are naïve and willfully so. The vigilant, fear-ridden paranoia required by my world is sacrificed by the Amish, right along with electricity and cars and household appliances and Guess jeans. The Amish say "no" to my world in an effort to reach for another kind of world.

Their schoolhouse had no metal detectors. No security guards tooting around campus in golf carts. No barbed wire and chain-link fences. No soda machines in cages. Just a sign that said "Visitors Welcome."

Evil was the visitor.

When evil or other tragedy comes to visit, human beings must recalculate the great equation of Sensibility, Fear, and Freedom:

Yes, the world contains danger.

Yes, a thoughtful and moral person makes every reasonable effort to be cognizant of the dangers, and to reduce the vulnerability wherever possible.

Yes, fear is sometimes a rational, healthy, and appropriate response to danger.

Yes, most of our strategies for reducing risk and vulnerability cost us bits and pieces of our humanity, restricting our freedom to be our most contented selves.

Yes, it is hard to maintain a reasonable level of fear without that fear morphing into a way of life, and thereby robbing us of life.

We enter the data piece by piece in our individual or collective human data banks, and we decide how we shall then proceed. How will we live? Who will we be?

What would best honor the lives of the dead Amish children? Adding fences and metal detectors and security guards to the schoolhouse? Or turning right around and reopening that schoolhouse, just like it was, with an even bigger sign out front saying "Visitors welcome"?

I find myself rooting for the latter.

I moved here in 1996, and bought a home in North Las Vegas. But my real estate agent was loathe to travel north on Martin Luther King Boulevard, preferring to take a circuitous route to the east and around the area where she said "the poor blacks live." I pondered for a moment the idea that poor black people are inherently more dangerous than affluent black people. Then I asked her if she liked bowling. (I come from the Mel Brooks School of Social Intervention: One idiot prejudice deserves the parody of another.)

A few months later I took my two sons, then ages five and three, to City View Park. We slid down this huge slide. We played "cheetah and gazelle." We pretended the climbing apparatus was a space ship. As we walked toward the car, we approached an older black man watching us thoughtfully. I smiled, nodded, said hello. He shook his head and said, "We don't get many white families coming to this park."

"Really," I said. "Why?"

"I guess they're afraid to come," he said.

And like a reflex I said, "I'm not teaching my sons to be afraid."

"All right then," the man said with a slow grin blooming on his face.

I drove home feeling good about life. My boys and I were regulars at the park.

And, the following spring, on a Monday morning, I read in the newspaper that, on Sunday afternoon, two youths had fired shots into a six-year-old's birthday party. No one was hurt.

My sons and I had been playing Nerf football right next to that birthday party. We'd left the park about thirty minutes before the shooting.

Sensibility, fear, freedom — I had to recalculate.

Common responses to pain of loss are not useful

We are defined fundamentally by our losses, not our celebrations, virtues, and victories. When we meet someone, we focus on what is present. But I'm thinking that the fast track to getting to know someone might be more well informed by what is absent. By what is missing. By what has been lost.

You wanna get to know somebody? Ask them about their greatest loss.

It reminds me of an art medium I saw at my son's high school. I'm ignorant of the name, but it amounts to a rigid, white board over which is a layer of black waxy substance. You "draw" your picture not by the colors or lines or brush strokes you put *on* the board; no, your picture emerges because of what you take *off*. The students scrape away the black wax to reveal more or less of the white beneath. The only way you recognize what the artist intends is by what has been lost.

It reminds me of Michelangelo's marble sculpting of David. Ol' Mikey doesn't carve King David; he hacks off the parts of the stone that aren't King David. We see King David only because of the rubble of broken marble lying on the floor.

Loss changes you. Shapes you. Perhaps more than any other factor, it makes you who you are.

Yet, in this culture, we talk about loss like we might talk about, oh, a chess opponent. Like if we just try hard enough and play it smart enough, we have the power to make the loss *not* a loss. Like there's no such thing as real loss, just the illusion of loss.

I have close friends whose twenty-four-year-old son is dead. Single-car accident. Head injury. Six weeks of coma. Just never came out of it. Many people were useful and supportive. Some were not. Here's a short list of not-useful things the not-useful people said:

"There must be a reason for this."

"His work on Earth was finished."

"Look for the gift in this."

"Someday you'll know why this had to happen."

"There is so much to celebrate about his life."

Please, the truth or falsehood of such utterances is not in question here. It's their usefulness. Such utterances distract us from the task of grief. They talk as if there might be an alternative to loss, an alternative to grieving.

There is no alternative to loss and grief — except for the denial of grief, which brings myriad unhappy symptoms of heart, body, and mind.

Early in the movie *Platoon*, a combat private is badly wounded in a fire fight. He lies screaming on the jungle floor. The pain is beyond imagining. But his screams might alert the patrolling enemy. So his command officer leans into his face and bellows, "Take the pain! TAKE the pain!" The private sucks in a breath . . . and stops screaming.

At some point, we take the pain. We stop being shocked and surprised by it. We quit screaming, not because it hurts any less, but because screaming is no longer useful to us. We make the pain a part of ourselves. With hope and commitment, the pain may become a creative part of us. A part of us worthy of respect. A part to be valued.

The pain of loss is not denied. It is accepted.

I've had a loss. The kind that changes you forever. Like having your arm ripped off in a bus accident.

Yep — I eventually will be fine. I'll learn to live without my arm, metaphorically speaking. I'll wow them at the rehab clinic with my commitment, my focus, how quickly I learn to use the prosthesis. And, sure enough, if I open my heart and endure in hope, I will in time acknowledge gifts that emerge from the loss. Perhaps I will someday say to someone, "If I hadn't lost my arm, I would have never met you," or, ". . . I would never have this depth of character," or, ". . . I would not have this compassion and empathy," or ". . . I would have missed this experience."

Yeah, I'll be fine. But when I'm an old man, getting ready for bed, fumbling to unharness this bionic contraption for which my fluid and expert use has made me the reigning darling of amputees everywhere . . . well, I reserve the right to miss my arm.

And I'll still wish the accident had never happened.

Finding the right words to say to sad people

Two weeks ago, the *Review-Journal* published my column titled, "Common responses to pain and loss are not useful." Two things make me want to revisit that column now.

First, in the column I used an analogy regarding loss. I said it was "LIKE (emphasis mine) having your arm ripped off in a bus accident. I said I would "learn to live without my arm, METAPHORICALLY SPEAKING."

And I feel terrible, because four of you e-mailed me and one of you sent me a lovely card expressing compassion and condolences about the actual loss of my actual arm. It was an analogy. I am not in fact a physical amputee. I'm terribly sorry to have provoked this idea in the goodness of your heart. And, if five of you actually wrote to me with this misunderstanding, I worry there might be many more of you with this misunderstanding.

Second, I received a ton of appreciative mail thanking me for the column, and, in one way or another, asking me, "Well, then, what *do* you say to grieving people? What *is* useful?"

Fair enough.

Two things stop us from being useful to grieving people. These two things are often (but not always) related. The two things are:

1. Our unwillingness to take our own losses seriously.

2. The idea that love is helping people feel better — cheering them up.

Both of these problems are ego-driven. The first is an ego defense. If we are deeply committed to denying loss, sad people are a threat to our way of life. We try to talk people out of their pain (aka, cheer them up) to shore up our own tidy, illusionary world. The second is an ego aggrandizement. It makes us feel really good when a sad person says to us, "You really helped me feel better." (Sad people sometimes say this to not-useful friends just to get them to go away.)

It's no sin to have an ego. Both of these reactions are common, normal, and completely understandable. But if the question on the table is "how can I be more useful to sad people," then the answer will include our learning to subordinate our ego needs.

Don't explain it. Refrain from sharing your theories about why the universe is the way it is, why this sad person is suffering, why this loss happened, or why it "had" to happen.

Don't interpret it. Resist the temptation to tell the grieving person what this loss means, what this pain means, or what it could mean or might mean.

Stop helping them feel better. This strikes most people as odd. But think about it. If you were at the scene of a car accident, attending to a person weeping with the pain of their injuries, would you say, "There, there now, don't cry"? The only way to heal grief is to grieve. We are useful when we help people into and through their pain, and not very useful when we try to help them out of it.

The most important reminder I give myself when I'm helping a sad person is, oddly enough, *I don't know anything.* And because I don't know anything, I don't need the sad person to feel better. Or worse. I can respect them as a separate person. Then the chances are increased that I can be useful to them.

So, what do you say to grieving human beings?

I have mixed feelings about a suggested script. Because, of course, whatever you decide to say must come naturally from your own heart, personality, and communication style. Nonetheless, here's a sample primer of things that often come out of my mouth in the face of grief:

I'm here.

It hurts this bad.

Here come the tears.

Good job.

Don't stop crying.

Take the deepest breath you can.

This deserves your tears.

Pour it out.

Your tears are holy.

Your heart is breaking.

This is so hard.

Keep breathing.

Can you sleep?

Are you eating?

Are people helpful?

Who is helpful?

Do you have someone to talk to?

It doesn't make sense.

What a waste.

I'm SO sorry.

I know you're suffering.

Your pain matters.

I'm still here.

It's hard to behold the soul agony of another human being. Especially if you love that human being. Especially if you have developed the habit of dodging your own agony.

When you lose a child, grieving is a lifelong experience

When our first child is born, a loud voice says, "Runners, take your marks!" We hear the starting gun and the race begins. It's a race we must win at all cost. We have to win. The competition is called, "I'll race you to the grave." I'm currently racing three sons. I really want to win.

Not everyone wins.

I'm here at the national meeting of Compassionate Friends, an organization offering support and resources for parents who lose the race. I'm wandering the halls during the "breakout" sessions. In this room are parents whose children died in car accidents. Over there is a room full of parents of murdered children. Parents of cancer victims are at the end of the hall. Miscarriages and stillbirths are grouped together, as are parents who have survived their child's suicide. And so it goes.

In a few minutes, I'm going to address Compassionate Friends. This is the toughest audience of my life. I mix with the gathering crowd, and a woman from Delaware glances at my name tag. Her name tag has a photo of her deceased son. My name tag is absent photos. "So . . . you haven't . . . lost anyone," she says cautiously.

"My three sons are yet alive, if that's what you're asking me," I say gently. She tries to nod politely, but I can see that I've lost credibility in her eyes. She's wondering who invited this speaker, and what on Earth he could ever have to say to her.

My address is entitled "The Myth of Getting Over It." It's my attempt to answer the driving questions of grieving parents: When will I get over this? How do I get over this?

You *don't* get over it. Getting over it is inappropriate goal. An unreasonable hope. The loss of a child changes you. It changes your marriage. It changes the way birds sing. It changes the way the sun rises and sets. You are forever different now.

You don't *want* to get over it. Don't act surprised. As awful a burden as grief is, you know intuitively that it matters, that it is profoundly important to be grieving. Your grief plays a crucial part in staying connected to your child's life. To give up your grief would mean losing your child yet again. If I had the power to take your grief away, you'd fight me to keep it. Your grief is awful, but it is also holy. And somewhere inside you, you know that.

The goal is not to get over it. The goal is to get on *with* it.

Profound grief is like being in a stage play wherein suddenly the stagehands push a huge grand piano into the middle of the set. The piano paralyzes the play. It dominates the stage. No matter where you move, it impedes your sight lines, your blocking, your ability to interact with the other players. You keep banging into it, surprised each time that it's still there. It takes all your concentration to work around it, this at a time when you have little ability or desire to concentrate on anything.

The piano changes everything. The entire play must be rewritten around it.

But over time, the piano is pushed to stage left. Then to upper stage left. You are the playwright, and slowly, surely, you begin to find the impetus and wherewithal to stop reacting to the intrusive piano. Instead, you engage it. Instead of writing every scene around the piano, you begin to write the piano *in*to each scene, into the story of your life.

You learn to play that piano. You're surprised to find that you want to play, that it's meaningful, even peaceful to play it. At first your songs are filled with pain, bitterness, even despair. But later you find your songs contain beauty, peace, a greater capacity for love and compassion. You and grief — together — begin to compose hope. Who'da thought?

Your grief becomes an intimate treasure, though the spaces between the grief lengthen. You no longer need to play the piano every day, or even every month. But later, when you're eighty-four, staring out your kitchen window on a random Tuesday morning, you welcome the sigh, the tears, the wistful pain that moves through your heart and reminds you that your child's life mattered.

You wipe the dust off the piano and sit down to play.

Values Matters

I VALUE TRUTH AND BEAUTY, IN NO PARTICULAR ORDER. Because truth is beautiful, and nothing can remain beautiful for long that isn't true.

I value respect for human dignity. Respect is from the Latin *respectus*, and means "to see again." Dignity is from the Latin *digne*, and means "the breath of God." To respect human dignity is to remember how easy it is for me to see people as an "it" or a "thing" — as a means to my end. So I see them again. I see them breathing the breath of God.

Remarkable. All you have to do to have a legitimate claim on me treating you respectfully is . . . breathe.

I value radical responsibility. Mercy. Letting people save face. Not hitting children. Not degrading children. Respect for animals and the earth. Taking a stand against evil. I hate bullies.

See, like everyone else, I have a cherished list of values. My values inspire me. They are a beacon of light. A way of living — or striving to live — for which I respect myself.

But values can't make us good.

My parents would often say it when I left the house to visit a playmate or when they dropped me off with my grandparents for a visit: "Be good." Their tone was not ominous — rather, encouraging. Cheery. And my response to their admonition was reflexive and enthusiastic: "I will!"

I was well into adulthood before I really examined this culturally scripted exchange. Suddenly the whole thing struck me as odd. What exactly did they want me to do? And what exactly was I agreeing to do?

Among my favorite prejudices about human beings is this: We cannot will our own goodness. I can't be good. I don't always even *want* to be good, which is one of the chief ways I know I'm not good.

Which isn't to say that I think human beings are bad. What I think is that we are born with instincts and comprehensive narcissism. We are not so much the center of the universe; we *are* the universe. One-year-olds never say, "Hey, when you get a minute, I'm a little hungry and my diaper is full. Don't stress. Next available is fine." Nope, babies scream bloody murder until the caregiver hops on over and makes the world a better place.

But if that's the way our children communicate instinctual discomfort at, say, age twenty-two, then we rightly take offense.

Have you noticed you don't have to teach children to be bad? You don't have to teach them to be aggressive or violent. You don't have to teach them to be obstinate, defiant, or disrespectful. Children require no instruction on deceiving or lying.

Children are born with a bundle of instincts. All of these instincts are designed for biological survival. None of them plays well for peace and harmony in the sandbox.

We don't punish infants and toddlers for instincts and narcissism. But we sure expect them to grow out of this primitive humanity into . . . into what?

I think most people in Western Civilization would say "into goodness." People should be good. We assemble collective and individual values for the purpose of instructing people to be good, and as a way of measuring when they fall short of goodness.

Our values commonly have much to do with "do this" and "don't do that." Do: love, forgive, defend the defenseless, give to the poor, work hard, tell the truth. Don't: smoke, drink, dance, play cards, lie, steal.

People will ask, "Does he have good values?" What does that mean? We have values about having values? Does it mean he has values just like yours?

Here's a great irony: The passionate pursuit of piety (being good) often leads diametrically away from the goal. It leads either to failure and self-loathing (we can't be good) or falseness (we lie to ourselves and others about how good we actually are) or dullness (we become miserably good) or rebellion (we get sick and tired of being good). Or it leads to hubris: We actually succeed in our pursuit of "goodness," and then we become insufferable. (If a holy person came over to my house for dinner, I'd have to invite another holy person over so the first person would have someone to talk to.)

Don't get me wrong. I'm all for effort. Trying to control our temper, trying to mind our tongue, trying to maintain self-discipline, struggling to change destructive habits — these are good things, and evidence of character. But it's important to remember that our best efforts will regularly fall short of goodness.

In its best moments, our relationship with goodness rests uneasy. As often as we welcome goodness with open arms, we also eye and posture with goodness like gunfighters at high noon.

True piety is a gift and a mystery. It's something for which we should give thanks. The mystery of goodness is every bit as mysterious as the mystery of evil. Sometimes I do the right thing because it is genuinely the thing I most enjoy doing. Sometimes I do the right thing while grousing and rolling my eyes, irritated with myself that I can't *not* do the right thing. Still other times I want to do that right thing, but some instinct (anger, greed, ego) erupts inside me and I'm truly surprised by my behavior.

Was that me? Did I say that? Yikes.

But what is really creepy is the way I can look an inferior choice right in the eye, know full well ahead of time that it's a waste of time, potentially destructive, or even guaranteed to hurt me ... and I choose it anyway. In truth, most of us don't often sin accidentally.

In the book *Sighing for Eden*, author Will Willamon asks an octogenarian Roman Catholic priest what he has learned in hearing sixty years of confessions. Without irony, the cleric says, "I have learned that human beings are far more miserable, and far less innocent, than they at first appear to be."

You gotta appreciate the candor.

Some values are clear, constant, and absolute. For example, I can't imagine any circumstances in which a woman should have to give up her right not to be raped or in which a child could rightly be beaten with a baseball bat. But more often our values are rife with contradictions and ambiguities. The crux of the moral life is dilemma. Life consistently requires us to choose between competing moral claims. It's agonizing.

We often teach our children to be good by teaching them to pretend, deny, and play-act. "I hate you," a child might shout in a fit of pique. Here, many parents mobilize classic admonishments:

"We don't say 'hate'!"

Yeah? If I can't say the word "hate," then how shall I talk when I feel hatred?

"You don't hate me. You're very angry with me."

Nope. It's pretty much hate — the shadow side of love.

"It's wrong to hate."

Okay then, have it your way. In addition to feeling hatred, I'm also a bad person.

"Now, now — you really love me."

You're saying you'll call me "good" if I become skilled at hiding my true self and pretending to be someone else? You're kidding, right?

Our ardent value is "not hating." But why wouldn't we value teaching people how to confess their hatred, and then how to manage those feelings morally and responsibly, how to ameliorate and transform those feelings into creative relationship, especially when it comes to rearing children? Instead, we inculcate self-delusion and call it character.

The psychological term is "splitting," and we use it to describe the way people chop off parts of the human experience and cast those parts into the shadowy darkness of the unconscious as the price they pay for the approval of parents and wider society. And the price is high. Splitting costs us psychic energy. It costs us integrity. It costs us wholeness and authenticity. It is at the heart of most compulsive behavior, depression, violence, and mental illness.

I talked to a woman once who said to me with no little pride, "I'm not perfect. I've made lots of mistakes. But at least I've never hurt anyone on purpose."

My response? Can't believe it came out of my mouth, but I couldn't stop it: "Really? On purpose is usually the *only* way I hurt people."

To never hurt anyone on purpose — this is an ego-wish. But it describes no human being I've ever met.

If you talk to me about values, I will relentlessly push you into the rigor of painful dilemmas and the work of emotional honesty. I'll make you uncomfortable. Real goodness inevitably flows from our acknowledgment of what isn't good within us. Goodness emerges as we are willing to acknowledge our limits and our brokenness.

In the end I'd rather be a human being than be good. Because I no longer trust goodness achieved by any other means. I value wholeness more than piety.

Understand mortality and you can improve your life

Play a game with me. It requires the use of your active imagination. It's like a guided fantasy.

Imagine a doctor tells you that you have ninety days to live. What?! The world caves in on you. The days following are filled with shock, terror, on-and-off denial. You wail. You cry.

But later, as things begin to stabilize inside you, as your mind clears, you begin to see your priorities. You begin the task of sorting out what is valuable and what is trivial. Which is mortality's specialty, by the way. Death has a way of floating what matters to the top.

Relationships are what matter.

In your imagination, look around at your circle of acquaintances, friends, and loved ones. There's someone you need to talk to. There's something you need to say to this person before you die.

Now, realistically, there probably are a lot of people you need to talk to, and a lot of things you need to say. But for the purposes of this exercise, pick one person. Just one. Let one face rise up in your consciousness.

Go to this person. Notice your surroundings. Are you in a home? On the patio of a coffee shop? Outdoors? Are you standing? Seated? In motion?

Who is this person? See him/her. Really focus. See the clothes, the hair, the eyes . . . especially the eyes. You have something you need to say to this person. It would be wrong to die and leave it unsaid.

Say it.

In your imagination, watch yourself say it. Hear yourself say it. Watch the person's face as you say it. Watch it go home to them. Imagine what they might say and do in response.

Play this scenario a couple of times, as you would replay a powerful scene in a DVD movie. Breathe it in. Breathe it out. Then, when you're ready, read on.

What did you say? I've offered this exercise countless times in a variety of psycho-educational or training groups. And over the years, what I notice is just how ordinary and common is the human experience. I'm saying people in this exercise tend to say the same sorts of things. Hands down, people tend to "say" one of the following four things:

"I love you."

"Thank you."

"Please forgive me."

"I forgive you."

People just aren't that different.

So, you might ask, what's the point of this exercise? What's the punch line?

We don't get to choose whether we die. But we do get to decide how. By "how," I don't mean the specific bio-organic interruption in our life force (cancer, coronary, car accident, embalmed by fast food, bored to death by celebrity gossip, etc.). By "how we die," I mean how we live with and into our mortality. How we decide to be related to death.

Of course, the most common way Americans die is pretending they won't. Ever.

But there's another way. It's not depressing. It's not a downer. Quite the opposite. It's at once humbling and exhilarating. Inspirational. Even peaceful.

We embrace it. We decide to know it. Our status as finite human beings (that is, human beings with only so much time) becomes the guiding light for our life choices. Mortality doesn't bring panic; rather, mortality brings acuity. A delicious urgency.

So, see the person's face again. In your imagination, say the thing you have to say.

The punch line?

Ask yourself what's keeping you from putting down the newspaper, going to the phone or e-mail and arranging to be in the same time/space coordinates with this person *now*. Soon. And saying the thing you need to say.

"Because nobody's told me I'm dying," says the young woman to me and the group last weekend. She says it with a straight face. As if she's made a point.

See, that's the problem with living in this culture. Nobody will tell you that you're dying. Sometimes it's even hard to get doctors to tell you.

"Let's fix that," I say gently to the nice woman. "You're dying."

Hearts and minds conflict over death penalty

I should tell you upfront that I am a life-long opponent of capital punishment.

Now, there are a variety of reasons one might assemble to be against the death penalty. Probably the most common argument I hear is the "deterrent" argument. Folks against the death penalty point out that capital punishment is not a deterrent to capital crime, that there is no evidence that increased executions can be linked to any decrease in murders. Folks for the death penalty point out that this is not the point, that all they care about is deterring this convicted murderer's capacity to murder again, which capital punishment accomplishes in spades.

But, for me, there is only one reason to oppose capital punishment: We're not very good at it.

It's been flat-out CREEPY how many death row inmates have been released in the last twenty years as the science of DNA evidence has emerged. I try not to let my brain float back over the past two hundred years, imagining just how many times the trap door dropped or Ol' Sparky roared, ending the life of an innocent human being. It's just not the sort of error that "Oops" can manage.

Okay, some might say, but now we have DNA evidence. Those mistakes shouldn't happen anymore. We'll send letters of commendation to the surviving families of the Oops Executions, and assure them that a grateful nation will never forget the sacrifice of those innocents who so bravely helped us refine our practice.

But naked human error is only one part of why we stink at capital punishment. The other issue is money. To whit: If you have lots and lots of money, the chances of you being executed go way, way down. If you don't have lots and lots of money, the chances of you being executed go way, way up. It's embarrassing.

So, I oppose capital punishment. It's beyond us. We can't do it fairly or accurately.

Then Timothy McVeigh bombed the Alfred P. Murrah Federal Building in Oklahoma City. If you know the story, it was blind luck that we caught him at all. But catch him we did. And try him we did. And we sentenced him to death. And then we killed him.

And I didn't blink. And this surprised me very much.

I came home from work early the day of the bombing. Turned on the TV. Sat mesmerized and weeping. Saw the now-famous footage of the police officer carrying a dead infant out of the rubble. Never got up to eat dinner.

"Why are you still *watching* this?" my wife asked incredulously some five hours later as she went to bed.

"I have to stay connected to these people's suffering," I said.

I finally did go to bed.

Months later, as McVeigh's execution date neared, the various mailing lists I inhabit regarding opposition to capital punishment began to fire messages onto my e-mail screen. And I stared at them. And then deleted them. I didn't attend any of the meetings. And when McVeigh died, I heard the radio report with all the interest of a man watching paint dry. Utterly detached. Empty.

I wasn't mad at Timothy. I was done with him. Couldn't mobilize a scrap of empathy. Couldn't locate my familiar indignation regarding the practice of the death penalty.

How surprising are the mysterious layers and contradictions of the human experience! If you ask my head, I'll tell you that the death penalty is immoral and unhelpful. I'm against it. If you ask my heart, at least as it regards certain capital crimes, it turns out I can wish you dead.

Gives one pause.

Relationship between being and doing is profound

The parenting experts tell us to separate our children's behavior from their identity. "I love you," we are supposed to say, "but I don't like what you are doing." In this way, so the theory goes, we can correct what a child is doing without shaming his being.

I am mostly a supporter of this strategy for discipline and change, whether it is used by parents or by individuals striving to confront their own mistaken behavior. Separating ourselves from our behavior is an effective way to break through the paralyzing shame many of us feel about both who we are and what we have done. Once we have regained power over shame, we are set free to celebrate our lives and take responsibility for our actions.

Alcoholics Anonymous, for example, uses this model to frequent success. In the AA model, alcoholism is not the name of an action (something we do) nor a reference to moral identity (someone we are); alcoholism is the name of a disease. Over and over I have seen this separation of being and doing give problem drinkers a way to climb out from under their shame and despair long enough to make the necessary changes for health and wholeness.

I say "mostly a supporter" because lately I've been thinking about the limits of this model. While it may be occasionally helpful to think in terms of separating identity and behavior, finally, no such separation really exists. We fool ourselves if we say that our behavior has no relationship to our person. If a man lies to me twenty times, and on the twenty-first occasion of our meeting tells me he is not, in fact, a liar, I will pause. I will doubt the man. If the man has fifteen convictions for theft, and tells me of many other thefts for which he was never discovered, I will not find much comfort in being told that, while his behavior is wicked, he is really a nice guy.

My car is rear-ended at a busy intersection. The guilty driver pleads with me not to call the police because he has no insurance and he wishes to avoid the additional citation. He assures me he has a friend at an auto body shop who will fix my car, and asks how he might gain my trust. I survey my damaged car. I see a man who has willfully rejected his legal and moral responsibility to carry insurance. Can he be trusted? He cannot. My answer is informed by his decision to drive without insurance. What he has done has told me something of who he is. I call the police.

The relationship between being and doing is profound. Each can change the other. When an evolution (or devolution) occurs in our being, then we do differently. When we practice some doing long enough (for good or ill), then our being moves to conform to the doing. Doing issues forth from being. Being is shaped by doing.

Of course, our doing is rarely a complete picture of who we are. Even in the midst of our most miserable acts there remains the part of our identity that knows the act was miserable. If we know we acted badly, then we can't be entirely bad. That's really good news.

But what we do remains a serious business. Our doing, if left unchecked and unexamined, has the power to blur and even bury our identity. Our character. To take seriously the connection between being and doing is to realize that at some point it is possible to no longer be doing evil, but to have finally become evil. Gives me the creeps.

Culture that denies death weakens life

Friends, colleagues, and readers ask, "So, you gonna write about Terri Shiavo?"

I was thinking "no." Plenty enough has already been written. The first thing I remember reading about Terri was published in 1818 by English novelist Mary Shelley. The book was titled *Frankenstein*. Not quite two centuries later, Terri Shiavo's tragedy was again addressed in Stephen King's horror novel *Pet Sematary*. And shortly thereafter, Michael Crichton reviewed the issue in *Jurassic Park*.

Or, if you prefer film, try *Johnny Got His Gun* (based on the Dalton Trumbo novel), the story of a war veteran come home alive, but without his limbs or his face. Can't talk. Can't see. Can't hear. No I.D. No one knows who he is. Medical technology saves him. But for what? The poor guy ends up banging his head against the pillow in Morse Code, tapping out his request to die.

Each of these stories is about the immutable boundaries of time and death, and about the universal human hubris that cannot and will not accept those boundaries. Each of these stories is about people who acquire the knowledge and power to trespass those boundaries, and the terrible sorrows that arise from the trespass. Each of these stories is about Terri Schiavo, her extended family, her husband, and the rest of us who watched in both horror AND fascination (come on, admit it) as the drama unfolded. Personally, I'm hoping to die with a little more privacy.

Terri's surviving sister, Suzanne Vitadamo, appeared on my television addressing the media with words of hope, forgiveness, and inspiration. Hers was a beautiful and well-crafted address. Deeply sincere and powerful. Then she said it: "My family and I thought this day would never come." And in my mind I said, "Oh lordy, girl — you didn't hear yourself just then, did you?"

Like some cosmic Freudian slip, Suzanne put her finger right on it: We are the characters in the above-mentioned stories. We think death won't come. We fight with it when it does come. When it should come. We think the only death worthy of us is the death we die while fighting not to die. I wish I had a nickel for every bereaved relative whose eulogy of their beloved included this proud assertion: "He/she never gave up!" Never gave up what, exactly? Trying not to be mortal?

It's not about giving up or not giving up, it's about surrendering to being human. The wife of a hospice patient once pulled me aside and asked, "Is there any hope?" The answer to her question depends entirely on what we hope in and for. Is there any hope that we can be immortal? Death-proof? No, there is no hope. Any hope that we can love anyone without suffering? No, there is no hope. But is there hope that mortals can live, love, suffer, and die in joy, peace, dignity, and meaning? There is always hope.

Pope John Paul II led several voices around the globe pointing to the Terri Schiavo saga as evidence that ours is a "culture of death." With all respect to the late Roman Catholic leader, I think there is in our culture a much more serious indictment to be made: Ours is a culture of death-denial. And the denial of death causes untold suffering. It is the enemy of joy and freedom — even morality.

Ben is my Paiute friend. He is a spiritual leader to his people. To me. We talked once of death. "You white people," he said with both compassion and puzzlement. "If you will let them go, you can have them back. But you will not let them go. Both suffer."

Take 'radical responsibility' for consequences of your choices

My fiftieth birthday turns out to be a portal of sorts — a movement through one time and one identity into the embrace of a new time and a new identity. It's fun, if sometimes uncomfortable. Freeing to definitively discard some old ways of being and old ways of seeing myself. A little strange to be meeting my own acquaintance.

My birthday is also an occasion to inventory values. "What really matters to you," a friend asks over birthday dinner, "and how has that changed since you were, say, thirty?"

What I notice more, actually, is the long and vestigial list of things that once mattered greatly. That people should like me. That I should have a lot of money. That my thriving depended on things being just and fair. That I had to examine myself constantly. That I deserved to be famous. That I would be more of a real man if I could overcome my fear of roller coasters, bungee jumping, and skydiving.

So many things, thankfully, no longer matter. The days are lighter because of that.

"You know the things I value," I told my friend. "Respect for human dignity, truth, beauty, and radical responsibility."

"I remember all but the last one," he says. "Is it a newcomer to the list? Tell me."

My interest in human responsibility has been around for a while, in pieces. But it's clearer now to me than ever that radical responsibility is a non-negotiable attribute in living well.

Radical responsibility has three parts:

The Intentional Life

The Intentional Life is life on purpose. It the conscious refusal of the accidental life — life as one continuous "oops." People who live intentionally spend more time proacting and interacting with life than they spend reacting to life.

The Intentional Life accepts that most of our life circumstance is directly or at least partly related to the sum of our choices — conscious and unconscious — over the course of moments or years. Few of us are as innocent as we first appear to be.

The Intentional Life acknowledges randomness and ambiguity. For example, some Canada backpackers have beheld the natural wonder of the mighty grizzly bear; other backpackers have been beheld by the might grizzly bear and been mauled or killed. If you hike in Canada, that happens sometimes, no matter how careful you are.

Even so, the Intentional Life embraces ambiguity intentionally! The Intentional Life is not surprised to find that life is surprising.

The Intentional Life is not the controlling life. Quite the contrary, the Intentional Life constantly assesses its own sphere of influence, and intentionally accepts the limits of that influence. It is a paradox: The Intentional Life intentionally submits to the implacable mysteries of life events. In conscious submission — not cynical resignation, not passive fatalism — we accept radical responsibility for all life circumstances, even circumstances beyond our control.

From Victim to Hero

To be victimized means to experience injustice or tragedy. To be "a Victim," however, is to confuse the events of injustice or tragedy with our very identity. To be a Hero is to take responsibility for our identity despite injustice or tragedy.

We are vulnerable to injustice and tragedy, and there are limits to our ability to defend ourselves. We can practice safety, use caution with strangers, lock our doors, practice healthy habits, and still things happen. We can be victimized.

But the power to decide how we are related to events, what the events ultimately mean, the power to decide who we are in the midst of those events — that power belongs to us.

Ethics

The radically responsible life is a commitment to a life of ethics. Ethics are not the same as morals. Morals have more to do with specific codes of conduct: "Do this. Don't do that."

The ethical life is first and foremost about our relationship to our conduct. Our conduct is ours. No amount of explanation for our conduct — even insightful and accurate explanation — changes the fact that our behavior belongs to us.

The Ethical Life has stopped arguing with the Cosmic Law that people make choices and choices have consequences.

Which leads me to the Pledge of Allegiance to Exceptional Living:

> "Here and now, I, _____, do pledge to take radical responsibility for all the consequences of all my choices, conscious and unconscious . . . even the consequences I neither expected nor intended."

Not saying I do it perfectly, but I like aiming for it. I admire people who reach for it.

You can't 'educate' racism out of existence

So I saw the movie *Crash*. I loved it. I hated it. Compelling. Sickening. At first glance, it's a movie about racism. But afterward, you realize it's about a problem much more serious than that: Something is wrong with us. By "us" I mean us human beings.

I belong to a religious organization whose national leadership decided its membership should undergo anti-racism training. We gathered, and the instructor directed us to the first page of our handbook. There in black and white (no pun intended) was the first curriculum tenant: "People are born good."

(If people were born good, anti-racism training wouldn't be necessary.)

Things would have gone smoothly if the instructor hadn't stopped right there and asked us what we thought of the first tenant. I didn't have time to call the Shut-up Police. Nope — there was my right arm reaching for the sky. "I think the first tenant is demonstrably untrue," I said, "and I know that because I'm a father."

If you have children and are paying attention, you notice that, when they are born, you don't have to teach them to be bad. Homo sapiens come out of the womb acquisitive, grabby, utterly narcissistic, and fully capable of violence. You don't have to teach them how to rage or hit or steal. You don't have to teach them to deceive or lie. We are born asserting ourselves and our instincts into the world, and heaven help anything or anybody (regardless of race, creed, or national origin) who stands in the way of the assertion.

None of this is to say that children are born bad, only that we are born utterly human. Hopefully you didn't punish your infant and toddler for primitive instincts and ego absorption; instead, you provided intervention, containment, distraction, soothing, and eventually modeling to teach the restraint of instincts and the emergence of character. That is, you taught your child to be good. Children aren't born bad . . . or good; they are born in a primitive humanity. And some time between birth and, say, age twenty-one, we expect them to grow out of their primitive humanity into another kind of humanity.

Except that none of us (of any race, creed, or national origin) ever truly grow out of the primitive humanity. Inside of us is a trembling, frightened, insecure ego, always looking for some way to assert itself and be comforted. Racism is only one way — a particularly pernicious and ghastly way — to assert the ego . . . the false self. If I attach my ego to a race or a tribe or a culture or an ideology, I can put off the ego-death of emptiness or ordinariness. I'll be somebody.

Identity by negation: I'm not black. I'm not gay. I'm not a woman. I'm not a Minnesota Vikings fan (probably could have left that out). And *voila*, my world is now safe and tidy. Racism (any kind of bigotry, actually) is a kind of maintenance of my safe and tidy world. A reconnaissance. I reach out to disdain, condescend, abandon, oppress, or even to exterminate people deemed inferior as a strategy to be somebody. You AREN'T, therefore I am.

It's impossible to educate someone from racism to not-racism. The same way it's impossible for the surgeon general's warning to stop people from smoking. People don't smoke because they are ignorant of the dangers. And people aren't racist because they have the wrong information about other races. We practice the habit of racism because it's comforting to our anxious and fragile (and false) ego-identities. It saves us from the unnameable (and largely unconscious) terror that we might be nothing.

A racist doesn't need an education. A racist needs a conversion experience. In the movie *Crash*, some people find their conversion experience. Others don't.

Psychological explanations don't always 'explain' our actions

Vocabulary word of the day: epistemology. It's the study of how we *know* what we know.

For example, the epistemological argument for the idea that sea lions bleed when Great White sharks bite them is, well, very strong. We know that we know that because we have it on film. But the epistemological argument for the idea that you bite your nails because your mother had ambivalence about breast feeding is not so strong.

See, a curiosity about my profession is a therapist's presumption to explain things. That's the popular role of psychology in our "psychologized" culture. Us therapists explain things. And we do so without a lot of regard to sound epistemology.

Why do I [fill in the blank]?

Unsuccessful attachments. Failure to differentiate. Passive father. Critical mother. Bad potty training. Found dad's *Playboy* stash. Mother was a drunk. Permissive parents. Rigid, critical parents. Cruel parents. Too much TV. Forced to eat lima beans. Traumatized by clown at circus.

We got a million of 'em, folks. And we've so saturated this culture with the language of explanatory diagnosis that we've got you doing it, too.

A woman talks about her past. Specifically, her past behavior with men. "I have this driving need for affection because my mother gave me insufficient affection," she says.

She's certain that her behavior with men is driven by a need for affection which, in her mind, is excessive compared with other folks' needs for affection. She concludes, then, that there must be something wrong with her particular need for affection, and the thing that's wrong is a deficiency in her mother's parent skills. With this knowledge, she can "fix" the thing that's wrong.

She seeks to explain her behavior. But the explanation doesn't explain. There are at least three ideas in her "knowledge" that she couldn't possibly know that she knows.

So I ask her: What's the right amount of need for affection? How are we certain that your enjoying and seeking the attention of men is a pathology? Why couldn't it be really normal and a whole lot of fun? And, if your behavior wasn't fitting your values, or if you didn't like the consequences, why wouldn't you simply conclude that not everything fun is good for you — and then stop. Why would the behavior need to be explained by someone's deficiency — yours or your mother's?

What if your very need to explain (and pathologize) your behavior is the real problem?

A specialty of mine is suicidology. That means I spend time with survivors of suicide. Unspeakable grief. I notice how quickly these families and friends grasp for a reasonable explanation. Phil was depressed. Phil's wife left him. Phil lost all his money in the stock market. These explanations do not lessen the pain, but they bring a facsimile of sanity to the bereaved.

Yet, in the privacy of my mind, I struggle. Not all depressed patients kill themselves. Not all discarded spouses kill themselves. Not all unlucky stock traders kill themselves. These explanations do not explain.

"Okay, smarty-pants," says my Voice Within, "then why is Phil dead?"

And the answer was so clear and so stark and so difficult. Phil is dead because, in a given moment, he lost the will to live and pulled the trigger. Who could blame the bereaved for seeking comfort in other explanations?

Why did John and Cathy get a divorce? Because Cathy gained a lot of weight. Because John had an affair (which he "explained" by pointing to Cathy's weight). Because Cathy would never go camping. Because John won't vacuum.

These explanations don't explain. A lot of people *don't* divorce in these circumstances.

Of course some divorces are necessary. Even desirable. But the majority of divorces happen because, in a given moment, one or both parties lose the will to be married. Someone goes to a lawyer and pulls the trigger.

I'm suspicious of our use of psychology to explain things. I wonder how often our explanations are accurate. Or how we could ever know if they are accurate. But more often I wonder if our presumed explanations don't mostly provide a cushion from the breathtaking burden of radical responsibility for our own lives.

Our choices are ours. That's where wellness begins.

Society misses the true meaning of integrity

Ask just about anyone for a definition of integrity, and they'll talk about being honest. Not lying. Telling the truth. Which is odd, because honesty is an inadequate synonym for integrity. It's not what it means at all.

About the only people who use the word literally anymore are carpenters and engineers. You'll see woodworkers at Home Depot, holding a two-by-four up like a rifle, turning and weighing the board in their hands. They are looking for integrity. After a bad storm, an engineer will inspect a building and say the integrity of a beam or girder has been compromised.

Integrity has little to do with truthfulness, and much to do with relatedness. The word in Latin is *integra*, and means "inner strength." Integrity refers to the inner strength yielded by the way the parts of things are related to the whole. A two-by-four has integrity when the wood grain layers and occasional knot are so related as to yield the strength of the whole board. A building has integrity when the various girders and beams are so related as to make the structure want to stand rather than collapse.

As human beings, we have integrity when the myriad aspects and attributes of our humanity are properly related within ourselves. When we are properly related, we find inner strength, and authentic action proceeds.

For example: All of us possess the human instincts of hunger, thirst, fear, sex, intimacy, autonomy, aggression, etc. And none of these instincts has a moral value. That is, we're wrong to call them good or bad. Instincts are simply human. It is the way our instincts are related to the whole of ourselves that determines our integrity. When instincts are properly related in service to our human wholeness, we thrive. We have integrity. But when we live to serve our instincts, we disintegrate. We are weakened or even harmed. Eventually we will harm others, too.

Likewise our thoughts and feelings require integration. Everyone has big ideas. Everyone has profound feelings. But both logic and emotion are seductive, because neither thinking nor feeling can, in the end, embrace the entirety of the whole human experience. Not everything we feel is useful or even true. Relying on logic at all costs is, in the end, illogical. Both thinking and feeling need to be integrated into a bigger picture of reality.

So, how is truth-telling related to integrity? I'll be the first to admit that lying will more often than not undermine our integrity.

Yet, truth-telling does not guarantee our integrity. Sometimes our truth-telling issues from a lack of integrity. An inappropriate exposure. A cruelty or exploitation. As a favorite author of mine says, "If you always tell the truth because honesty is the best policy, then your honesty is corrupt."

I was lucky once to acquire backstage passes to a performance by one of my favorite singer-songwriters. She's the daughter of a theologian, and her lyrics consistently blow me away. Now I would have the chance to meet her in person.

We met. She was lovely and personable. I asked about a line in my favorite song of hers. She told me it was derived from an English poem. Then I asked her about the song itself. What inspired it?

"I made it up," she said simply.

And she was lying. I swear she was lying. I didn't believe her then, and I don't believe her now. I *am* a songwriter. All profound art — even fiction — is attached somehow to the biography of the artist.

But of course she lied. It was good and right for her to lie. Because it was a boorish, intrusive, insensitive question. Like, I'm sure she's gonna tell her intimate life story to some fan geek.

Her lie came from a place of integrity.

Our prudish tendencies don't fit every situation

Fair warning: This column might make some of you uncomfortable. If it's any consolation, I'm a little woozy myself.

I was in Las Vegas for maybe a year when I was stopped at a light on Paradise Road, somewhere north of Flamingo Road. My two sons, then six and four, looked up to a billboard. There was the signature pose of the *Crazy Girls*. Arm in arm. Bare backs. Big hair. Thongs. My children erupted in gales of laughter. "Look, the butt sign," they giggled gleefully.

Uh, yeah, boys. The Butt Sign. Not much arguing with that.

Now, I promise I'm whatever the opposite of a prude is. As a student and observer of history and anthropology, I have tried to wrap my mind around the phenomenon of the modern — what to call them — professional naked person? From nude stage shows to strippers to actual prostitutes: Who are these people? In one form or another, they've been around since the dawn of civilization.

Is it mere debauchery? Does that explain it from top to, uh, bottom? Or is it possible to enter this work as true vocation? Is there such a thing as choosing a career in corporate erotica? Can it ever be art? Ever be a contribution to humanity? Or is it only pathology?

No matter how I try to open my mind to a deeper picture, there are disturbing realities. A ton of the women in these professions are childhood sex abuse victims. A ton. Are they celebrating erotica and human sexuality? Or are they acting out the drama of their own psychic wounds? If it is the former, that's one thing. If it is the latter, I'd feel a little creepy participating.

Is there a scenario in which I could be relaxed and accepting — let alone proud and admiring — of my daughter as phone sex worker or stripper or prostitute? (These women are all somebody's daughters.) Does this industry make for joy and vitality in the human race? Is it ever a real celebration between a man and a woman? Or is it a ceremonial hostility, an expression of an ancient fracture between the genders?

And then I had lunch with a mutual acquaintance of a dead friend.

Ray (not his real name) was born bright and strong and full of life. At age twelve, Ray was diagnosed with juvenile rheumatoid arthritis. By age fifteen he used crutches. By age nineteen, canes. Well into his twenties, he walked bent over, looking at the ground. The disease ravaged him without mercy.

Somehow, Ray managed to acquire a master's degree. He worked steadily throughout his adult life. He was a football fan. Learned a little guitar.

Ray died right around his thirty-eighth birthday, alone in his home. His father found him. It was over. In the end, he had arthritis in his *eyes.*

It was two years later I caught up with Ray's close friend. I don't know why he told me what he did. But he did. He said that, in the last years of Ray's life, a woman came to visit Ray now and again.

Two, maybe three times per year. The same woman. A professional woman. The woman attended Ray's funeral.

It caught me off guard. But then, what's even more startling is that I would be startled. A never-married man, a man who never had a real dating life, a man trapped by a senseless disease inside the tormented shambles of his human form — what in me had so easily and automatically dismissed and forgotten this man was still a sexual being?

But my final surprise was my thoughts and feelings about the woman. I imagined meeting her. And the words that would pour out of my mouth startled me about me. The words would not fit my acculturated values, or even the majority of my experience.

I would thank her. I would thank her for being nice to my friend in his short and too-cruel life. I guess I would be saying I was glad for her and her chosen profession, the way you'd be glad if you found just the right plumber, or doctor, or barber, or mechanic.

And I don't know what to make of that. Sometimes life just won't fit into any given box.

Anonymity brings out the worst in human behavior

There is Ugly in every human being, including the guy who writes this column. Some folks call it the dark side. It's the part of us that is compelled by carnage, fascinated by trauma, tempted and drawn to exploitation, and capable of enjoying (yes, I said "enjoying") the suffering of others.

A friend of mine once said, "I know I've hurt people in the past, but at least I have never hurt anyone on purpose." And I said, "You're kidding me, right? I mean, 'on purpose' is pretty much the only way I ever hurt people." Our impulse to hurt others might or might not be conscious, but either way the consequences of our actions are rarely an accident.

Anonymity makes The Ugly come out.

They showed us a film in my undergraduate psychology program about a now-famous post-World War II psych experiment wherein students were hired to ask questions of subjects sitting in a booth.

The student and subject were separated only by a glass. Each could see and hear the other. If the subjects answered incorrectly, the student flipped a switch giving the subject ever-increasing levels of electric shock. The student thought the experiment was about the cognitive capacity of subjects under threat of punishment. But the real subject of the experiment was the student.

With full visual contact, the students became more and more reluctant to flip the switch. Even when cajoled and demanded of them, students would quit the experiment before continuing to cause pain to the subject. But when visual contact was prevented by a drawn curtain, the students' willingness to dish out suffering increased dramatically, even when they could hear the (obviously staged) moaning of the subject.

Anonymity brings out The Ugly in us.

Automobiles provide the perception of anonymity, and this explains a large part of the phenomenon known as "road rage." The perceived anonymity that allows a driver to leisurely explore his nose with his finger at a stoplight is the same anonymity that allows for shaking fists and tailgating and obscene gestures from people who would never behave this way anyplace else.

And don't I love anonymous letters to the editor! Cowards, every last one of you. Hate my column, but don't expect me to answer your letter unless your John (or Janet) Jacob is affixed clearly to the bottom of the page.

Ever ask yourself why members of the Ku Klux Klan don veiled party hats before commencing their evening's activities? Why and how the Internet has vastly increased the consumption of pornography by otherwise "perfectly normal" middle-class Americans? Why and how cyberspace has awakened criminal sexual exploitation of minors in the lives of people in whom it might have otherwise remained a dark and permanently unspoken fantasy?

It's because, with anonymity, we *can*.

There's even a kind of anonymity associated with being a columnist. Not once have I ever been recognized in public as the Steven Kalas who writes *Human Matters*. The written word provides a distance between me and the reader that allows more anonymity than in my life as a professional public speaker. I often spend minutes on end editing my column for undue anger, snobbishness, contempt, glee, and the constant temptation to use this space to — well, might as well say it — enjoy humiliating folks who I think deserve it.

Didn't say I was proud of it. Only that it's true.

If anonymity provokes The Ugly, then accountability restrains it. The willingness to be accountable is the willingness to be seen. To be known. Accountability promotes healthy shame, and healthy shame provides the borders within which Ugly is bridled and decency may emerge.

There is no meaningful definition of relationship that does not include accountability. I once heard a husband complain, "Why should I have to tell my wife where I am and what I'm doing and when I'm coming home?" And I wanted to blurt out, "Because you're married, goofus! You're accountable! You agreed to be seen and known by this woman for the rest of your life!"

I once saw a bumper sticker that said, "Do the right thing even when no one is watching." Nice sentiment. But I prefer the follow-up bumper sticker: "And, when in doubt, make damn sure that someone is watching."

It really is more satisfying to give than to receive

When I was a boy, I could live and die seven lifetimes between Thanksgiving and Christmas Day. Time passed slowly in that thirty days, as if it was moving through Jell-O.

And all because of the promise of presents under the tree. Specifically, presents for *me*. My toys, my surprises, my loot, my take — it's all I could think about. It's a scientific fact that anticipation clogs the mechanism in clocks. Come to think of it, it might actually clog the whole solar system. Makes planet Earth rotate and orbit sluggishly.

I was eighteen and home from college one Christmas morning when I first noticed the change. It was the last Christmas I would spend in the house of my boyhood and youth. I'm sitting on the hearth, next to a happy fire. My little sister is being "Santa," passing out presents. A gathering of packages grows at my feet. My stash.

The change I notice is my relative disinterest in my stash. I'm much more interested in a particular package over in my mom's pile of presents. The gift I bought for her. I'm smiling about the package I wrapped for my sister. And my other sister. My birth father is there, too. Finally. Celebrating his first Christmas with me. His boy.

What has changed on this, my nineteenth Christmas, is the source of my greatest anticipation. For the first time in my life, I'm aware that I simply CAN'T WAIT for my loved ones to open the gifts I gave *them*! I want to see their faces. My sisters and I pretty much have a contest every year to see which of us can make our mother cry. (To be truthful, it's not that hard. Sorta like shooting fish in a barrel. Photographs usually work, or any gift that's hand-made, or any sentence that begins, "Hey, Mom, remember that time when we . . .")

As the years went by, I found myself becoming more and more impatient with the question, "Steven, what do you want for Christmas?" I didn't want to think about it. Whatever. Big box of cheese. Beck's beer. Junior Mints in my stocking. Underwear. Socks. Terrific red wines I'm too cheap to buy for myself. Movie passes. Stephen King books. Anything related to the Beatles. I want the same things EVERY year.

And who cares? I want to know what YOU want for Christmas!

Does anybody remember the Warner Bros. cartoon characters "The Goofy Gophers"? They are consummate gentlemen. Ultrapolite. Good manners *qua absurdum*. They start to raid the farmer's garden, look up, and see a cat bearing down on them. They run like mad to the gopher hole, stop, and begin an argument about who should go first. "After you" . . . "No, no — after you" . . . "I went first last time" . . . "I couldn't possibly" . . . "Please" . . . "Be my guest" . . .

And so it goes until one of them looks up and says, "Pardon me, but the cat will be here in a few moments, and I fear that if we don't resolve this dilemma shortly, we shall both be eaten." Finally they agree to hold hands and jump together.

Funny how even our desire to be generous and kind and loving can be conscripted in service to our ego.

I talk to a husband and wife struggling with sexual courtship. But they are not arguing about what each is not able to *get*. They are arguing about their frustration in trying to *give*. They have grown a love so great that now their greatest joy is found not in their own pleasure, but in rocking their mate's world. In the first years of marriage, they learned how to give. Now, eight years later, they find themselves called to offer each other a new sacrifice: learning to receive. They are surprised to find the new lesson requires an even greater depth of character than the first.

You've heard the ol' wise saying, "It's better to give than to receive"? Well, that's only half of the wisdom. The other half was lost for centuries in a shipwreck, recently salvaged. Joined again after all these years, polished and restored on display at the Smithsonian, we see this teaching as it was intended: It's better to give than to receive. It's also a whole lot easier.

The ultimate irony of learning the joy of loving selflessly is then hearing the criticism, "Hey, my turn to be generous and giving and doting. Stop hogging the unselfishness!"

Humility is understanding that we're in this together

"Be more humble, Steven."

This had to be one of the more constant mantras of my childhood and youth. More than just a relentless message from my parents, it was everywhere! The adults who raised and cared for my generation seemed to have one driving ethos, one overriding measure of whether they were faithful parents and good leaders of children: Whatever else you do, make sure your children don't think too highly of themselves.

It was, like, the worst imaginable outcome. The Eleventh Commandment: Thou Shalt Not Celebrate Thyself.

It took me until about my fortieth birthday to realize what should have been obvious: None of the people admonishing me to be humble had the slightest idea what humility was. Their definition came out "in the wash" something like:

"Steven, we'll call you humble if you pretend not to know what you know, if we don't catch you having too much fun being yourself, if you won't articulate any moments of deep satisfaction in excellence, if your gifts never force us to face our own envy, if, whenever anyone does offer a word of gratitude or praise, you pretend to be surprised at your own competence or maybe even chastise and correct the person praising you, reminding him/her that 'anyone could have done it' or that 'you were just lucky.'"

The Aw Shucks School of Humility.

Nobody tried harder than me to live into this definition. And frankly, (at the risk of thinking too highly of myself), I think I largely succeeded.

Which is why, I think, those same people hoping I'd be "humble" then accused me of being phony.

(Here insert the sound of maniacal laughter.)

Ever hear two women talking in reference to another woman across the room? "She's beautiful, but she knows it."

Yeah? So? Why shouldn't she know it? Would you say about Bill Gates, "He's a billionaire, but he knows it"? Would you say about Michael Jordan, "He's a great basketball player, but he knows it?"

If you are in possession of some gift — and beauty is the name of a gift — affording you a disproportion of power and therefore responsibility, shouldn't you know it? And, better yet, what if you could both know it and enjoy it?

The thing I hope the most for Michael Jordan, seeing as how he was the best basketball player ever in the known universe, is that he knew it. And enjoyed it. Enjoyed being himself. Because I enjoyed him immensely. It was nice of him not to demur, hold back, or pretend to be someone else.

Hiding your light from the world isn't humility. It's a joke. A game. A manipulation. And we try to pass it off as virtue.

On Palm Sunday, I think we make a mistake to assume Jesus chooses a donkey for transportation because he is humble. What

Jesus is is a brilliant satirist. Pilate enters Jerusalem through the west gate riding a decorated stallion. So Jesus makes a point by riding in through the east gate on a burro. And when the people shout "hosanna," religious folks (why am I not surprised) say, "Tell them to stop that! It's not humble!" And Jesus, in possession of true humility, says, "I suppose I could, but then the rocks would just start singing."

If I have to choose (thank God, I don't) between raising painfully aggrandized, insufferably narcissistic children, and children who live in a posture of constant, crippled apology and self-consciousness for their brilliance and beauty . . . well, I'll choose the former. My reasoning is simple: This ol' world has lots of opportunities to confront and shave off the rough edges of hubris. But damn few opportunities to heal and offer a hand up to people crippled by self-loathing, self-doubt, and fear.

My son walks out in a tuxedo. Tall. Dapper. "Geez, stud," I say, spontaneously. I drive him to school for his concert. Stopped at a light, I look over to the passenger side. My boy is holding back a canary-eating grin. His eyes dance and dart around. He looks like he's sitting on some delicious surprise, or really great news.

"What?" I ask.

He looks left, then right, as if to assure that we're alone. Then, face blushing, he whispers, "I look really good right now."

And I burst out laughing . . . not at him — this is my own joy erupting. It was so sincere, so bawdy, so earthy and real. It's fun to feel attractive and confident. And I'm so happy that he knows it. And is enjoying it.

The simple truth? He *does* look really good right now.

Humility is not pretending to be unaware of one's strengths and talents, nor is it restraining those same talents just so insecure people can feel less threatened.

So, what *is* humility?

It's a fair question. But defining humility is, for me, akin to defining love. A core definition eludes me. Rather, I end up delineating attributes and attitudes that may point to humility's presence.

Humility can be recognized by our commitment to **mutuality**.

I think of mutuality as a chosen worldview. An adopted attitude. Humility offers a median equanimity into the world. As I live my life, humility demands that I remain conscious of the fact that other people are living theirs. I belong on this planet no more and no less than other people belong. Mutuality means surrendering the fantasy that I am special, that I deserve to be afforded certain privileges just because it's me.

My father pounded this lesson when teaching me to drive, though he didn't use the word "humility." I came upon my turn sooner than expected, and found myself in the wrong lane. As I slowed to change lanes, thereby countermanding the forward progress of everybody behind me, my father told me to drive around the block and try again. "Where you're going, Steven, isn't more important than where any of these other people are going," he said. "Why should everybody else immediately stop what they're doing just because you're lost?"

Point taken.

Mutuality, in turn, gives birth to **hospitality**, the conscious practice of welcome and inclusion, solicitation and inquiry. If it's true that I am no more or less important than anyone else, then recognizing, welcoming, and including others becomes a way of life. When I bump into someone on Aisle 4 at the grocery store, I say, "Excuse me," which is shorthand for "I confess that, in my quest for Polish dill spears, I constructed my own special universe and lived for a moment as if I was the only person whose existence mattered. Turns out you and your grocery cart live in my universe, too. My bad."

Here the opposite of humility is entitlement and willful oblivion.

Humility is recognized by the **responsible use of power**. Or, as M. Scott Peck said in *The Road Less Traveled*, "The more power [healthy people] have, the more reluctant they are to use it." Humility acknowledges an ethos deeper than "'Cause I can." Humility asks more rigorous questions: Should I? Is it right? Is it fair? Is it the right time? Is it necessary? Is it useful? Or am I just showing off?

Humility self-deprecates and self-satirizes, which in no way means diminishing or degrading the self. Rather, humility is recognized in a playfulness with self that springs from the acceptance of one's common place in absurdity.

True humility makes a fair assessment of gifts and talents, enjoys them, but stops short of ego-identifying with those same gifts. We are not, in the end, summed up by our gifts. We are more than the sum of our attributes. Rich, tall, smart, pretty, Leading Passer Rating in the NFL — these are parts of us, but, alone, they are an insufficient identity. If all Michael Jordan knows of himself is that he's a really good basketball player, then he's in for a long and lonely retirement. Humility recognizes and embraces our talents, but ultimately reaches for something deeper upon which to build a meaningful life.

Humility lives out the twin formula "I am not nothing . . . I am not everything." It's a surrender to the ordinary. We're not special. We are in fact painfully predictable. Ordinarily human. We are born, we live, we eat, we sleep, we celebrate, we suffer, we die. The only thing remarkable is that we should live at all.

Even my narcissism is ordinary.

Growing up includes humble surrender to all we are and are not

A reader writes to ask: "**How does one get past regret? I have regrets from my childhood, my adolescence, and as a young adult. If only time travel were possible! I dream about how I would go back and do so many things differently, so that my life would be better today. I can't seem to get past the mistakes I made as a younger person.**"

Here's a fun parlor game: The Worst Thing I've Ever Done.

Ever played?

It tends to be played spontaneously — in hotel rooms or on late-night road trips. Maybe after most of the partygoers have gone home, and now it's just you and one or two best friends in a living room. The likelihood of this game goes up in direct proportion to the number of open wine bottles and empty beer cans in the room.

The game begins: "What's the worst thing you've ever done?"

Regrets fall quickly into three categories: missed opportunities, bad judgments, and moral regrets.

Missed opportunities

We miss opportunities because we can't or don't appreciate the open door before us. For example, I regret giving up on the guitar as a freshman in college. I wish I'd had the guts and the discipline to stick with it. I was thirty-three before I gave myself permission to be artistic and creative, to write and sing songs. What was I afraid of?

Want the truth? I've spent much of my life afraid of excellence.

We miss opportunities because we have egos as big as cathedrals and, paradoxically, as frail as butterfly wings. Especially in adolescence and young adulthood. Talking to youngsters about smoking, drinking, drugs, teen pregnancy, staying in school, choosing friends wisely, training for a meaningful career . . . well, sometimes it feels like this:

Grownup: "My best advice is don't deliberately hit yourself with all your might in the head with this sledgehammer. It will really hurt and you won't like it."

Youngster: "Yeah, what do you know? You can't tell me what to do!"

Our regret over missed opportunities really comes down to our embarrassing dismay over how long it took us to grow up, not to mention the growing up we still have left to do.

Bad judgments

We pick wrong. We're unlucky. Mostly we choose unwisely because we are not at the time in possession of sufficient wisdom. Instead of the new car behind Door #1, we pick the mule behind Door #2. And it's more than just the random failures of "betting on the wrong horse." More people than you could ever imagine come to regret the decision to divorce, change jobs, or relocate.

So, we're back to growing up, because, while facts and knowledge come in a box, judgment and wisdom come only with time.

Punishing and paralyzing ourselves for as-yet-unattained levels of maturity (growing up) is a bit like resenting not-yet-germinated wildflower seeds that lie slumbering in the desert sand. They grow and bloom when they grow and bloom. Not a moment before. Heaping contempt on the seeds doesn't make them grow and bloom any faster.

Moral regrets

Wish I had a nickel for every celebrity I've ever seen on a talk show who smiles a superior, enlightened smile, nods like the Buddha, and says meaningfully, "I have no regrets."

May I be frank? If you have no regrets, then take a hike. I don't want to know you. Because, while you might have been a "being," you've never been a *human* being. Human beings have regrets. Buckets of them.

What's the worst thing you've ever done?

I'll die ashamed of the way I treated my little sister when I was growing up. Oh sure, I can explain it clinically in the context of my family's systemic dysfunction. I was the Hero. She was the Scapegoat. Blah, blah, blah.

I was cruel to her because it assuaged my ego to be cruel to her. That she's forgiven me boggles the mind. An undeserved gift.

Here's where I'm supposed to take off on my "forgive yourself" speech, right? Wrong. Great if you can forgive yourself. But before that's even possible, we must tell ourselves the truth and accept that truth. The truth includes regret. Guilt. Sorrow.

Growing up includes a humble surrender to all we are and are not. The regrettable parts of our past become just as important as the laudable parts. Ironic treasures. Sources of surprising peace and wisdom. A tether for ego. A measure by which we appreciate the miracle of love and friendship.

You'll never hear me say, "I have no regrets." What I strive for is not having any regrets about my regrets.

I no longer apologize for being a human being.

Changing the stories you tell can be good therapy

All the great tales begin with it. All the best stories are thusly introduced. Countless times did my mother speak the familiar words as she read folk and fairy tales to me at bedtime:

"Once upon a time . . ."

And so we tell our stories. But it's not just stories read out of a children's book. Human beings tell stories about everything. We tell stories all the time. We never merely have an experience. We are compelled to tell a story about the experience.

It matters what stories we tell, because the way we tell our story shapes the way we integrate our experience, which in turn shapes what happens next. Our stories provide the stage for how we embrace our future. For better or for worse.

Consider a mom and a dad complaining about their teenage son's behavior. I might ask them what best describes their son. Should his face be on a wanted poster? Or on a March of Dimes poster? Two different stories, each calling for a different response. Is the boy more like a criminal, or more like a child with a handicapping condition?

Alcoholics Anonymous works by retelling an alcoholic's story. Most drunks tell a story something like, "I'm a bad, stupid person who drinks too much." AA tells a new story: "You're an alcoholic, which is the name of an incurable disease, which you can manage only with the help of a Higher Power."

When Sylvester Stallone did the *Rambo* movies, he retold the story of the Vietnam War. This time we win. Or should have. Could have.

Healthy religion tells a story: In the beginning. We were slaves in Egypt. There were shepherds watching their flocks by night. The people in darkness have seen a great light.

Unhealthy religion tells another story: God really likes you, and he's counting on you to oppress, exploit, or kill the people he doesn't like.

A woman in love tells a story like this: He's sensitive, empathic, and can talk about his emotions. He's so creative. A dreamer. Spontaneous and fun. But a divorcing woman tells a different story: He lacks ambition. He's weak and unmanly. The same man with the same attributes. But now a different story.

A man in love tells a story like this: She's a domestic dream. So organized. Runs the house like a Swiss watch. But a divorcing man tells a different story: She's a controlling bitch. The same woman with the same attributes. But now a different story.

If you haven't already noticed, we tend to tell our stories with an eye for convenience.

One way to think about therapy is to say a skillful therapist helps you tell better stories, stories that leave you more room in which to live whole and well. "I just don't know why I keep doing it," says the guilty husband caught in his third affair. See, he wants to tell a story of an inexplicable, psychological mystery. I offer an alternative story: "Maybe you do it because it's fun and you like it a lot."

Sometimes we need a merciful story. I find it particularly meaningful to help people tell stories of compassion to counter all-too-frequent stories of infamy and self-loathing. Very few people need help feeling bad about themselves.

Sometimes we need a brutal story, such as when the Man with the Terrible Temper says to me, "The way I treat people is horrible! I hate this part of me!" Sounds like a useful story to me. "Good for you," I say simply.

Sometimes we need one story for a while, and then grow out of the old story and need a new one. For example, when someone first admits to suffering child abuse, the usually tell a Tragic Story, a story of tears and helplessness, injustice and indignation. But after a time, that same person might trade the story of tragedy for the Hero Story, a story of endurance, survival, and personal transformation. The Hero offers his wounds back to the world as a healing balm and beacon of hope. The Hero absorbs violence, and now teaches beneficence.

And when you find your stories becoming dire and empty, as mine become sometimes, then I make something up. I try something on. Such as, once upon a time there was this forty-nine-year-old columnist/therapist who had yet to see the most beautiful part of his life. Don't know if I believe that story yet, but at least I'm willing to tell it.

Choose your stories carefully, because your stories can either set you free or pin you like an insect to a board. Your stories can promote depth, or condemn you to the netherworld of self-delusion.

Leave room in your stories to be surprised. Beware convenience. Be suspicious of stories that render you categorically innocent, because we are all non-innocents.

The best stories, of course, are the ones that are true.

Authenticity Matters

WHATEVER THEIR FELT OR STATED MOTIVE, PEOPLE ENTER DEPTH THERAPY TO FIND THEMSELVES, THEN TO GROW AND DEVELOP THE PERSON THEY FIND.

I wince saying that, because it sounds so cliché: "I've gotta go find myself."

I'm no respecter of the runaway train of collective narcissism that is this culture. There is a razor fine line between a laudable commitment to healthy self-discovery and narcissistic self-absorption. I'm bored with people who get divorces because they have to go find themselves. I've not much sympathy for twenty-four-year-old college dropouts who are unemployed because you just can't hurry the journey of vocational discovery. "It's just not a good time for me/us to have a baby" is a curious and troubling stand-in for moral deliberation about abortion.

I'm unconvinced that the behavior, tattoos, piercings, and hair dye of former professional basketball star Dennis Rodman constitutes especially courageous, authentic self-expression (though I'll die saying he was a preternatural defender and the greatest student and practitioner of rebounding I've ever seen).

Despite my mixed feelings, I notice how often I say to a patient: "I think our task is to find more of your*self*, and to strengthen your resolve to hold on to that self."

I call it the journey of authenticity. It is the singular passion of my life.

I think authenticity is the correct response to everything — the universal antidote for psychic malaise.

The Angry Young Man is referred to me. Age seventeen. I hear his big, black, waffle-stomping Gestapo boots coming down the sidewalk long before he turns the corner into view. He sports an eight-inch spiked mohawk. The sides of his head remind me of mirrors — so bald, smooth, and shiny.

Around his neck is a leather dog collar with metal studs. Through his nose is a silver loop attached to a chain that travels back to his left ear. His earlobes hang in tatters. Pierced tongue, lower lip, and right eyebrow. Two derelict motorcycle chains criss-cross his chest, bare except for the ragged sleeveless denim jacket. Both his jacket and jeans tout miniature, obscene graffiti.

"Why are you here?" I ask.

"People are afraid of me," he says without irony.

I shrug, nod, purse my lips as if we now agree on the obvious.

"*I'm* afraid of you," I say, nodding.

The Angry Young Man meets my eye. He's deciding, I think, whether to be offended, surprised, or intrigued: "You are?"

"Yep," I say blithely. "That's what you wanted, right? I mean, you don't accidentally dress this way, do you? It's designed to scare people, right?"

His was not a fashion statement, but an observable symptom manifested as anti-fashion. He felt angry and powerless, but he did not yet know he felt angry and powerless. So his intrepid unconscious devised a defense whereby he could shock and offend people while feigning as if not to understand why they were shocked and offended. The defense worked, after a manner, but at the cost of a deeper authenticity.

Our human race must sense and intuit the call to authenticity, even if most of us rarely consciously contemplate it. Else why would we have felt the need to coin the word "humane"? It seems there are beings, and then there are *human* beings. One way to tell the difference (according to our language) is the latter is observably humane.

It's "more human" to be nice to puppies than not to be nice.

That's the paradox: A human identity is both a given and a dynamic development. We are at once human and becoming human. While there are many different jobs and occupations to which we might offer our life's work, everyone is responsible for the universal vocation — the task of becoming fully and authentically human.

People cry over losses in therapy. Someone has died. A relationship has died. A particular time of life is fading. But there is one moment in most depth therapy guaranteed to evoke grief: the betrayal of self. The sudden realization — and it comes like falling suddenly through a trap door — that we have betrayed ourselves. We have lived falsely. Not authentically. We did not speak the truth, or our truth. Did not know our truth, and had willfully (if unconsciously) dodged the work of knowing.

We traded our self-respect for some lame facsimile of relationship or status or gain.

Admitting self-betrayal can be the beginning of dramatic human transformation. After the initial tears, remorse, and appropriate self-reproach, many people draw a proverbial line in the sand. They make new commitments to self and self-respect. They resume the journey of authentic living.

I should warn you, though. As we draw closer to authenticity, two things happen — one good and one problematic.

The good thing? The development of an authentic self taps into our real power and authority. People with a firm grasp on their identity have a solidity. A resilience. They are vital and real. Substantive. Dynamic, yet constant. Authenticity opens the flow of "life force" (libido). It is very powerful.

The problem? Well, simply put, authentic people tend to scare the holy horse hockey out of the rest of us. Authenticity inspires us and evokes our admiration, yes, but it just as often provokes our fear, insecurity, and envy. I once said it this way in a song lyric:

Well they say 'be yourself'
But they're just teasing

The self you must be
Is the one who is pleasing
To the folks who prefer
The you who just pretends
They call themselves family and friends
Some fences will never mend

Authenticity is a threat to people committed to a course of denial about their own emptiness. The reaction to this threat ranges from childish to homicidal. It can quickly turn ugly.

Wrap your mind around this: Gandhi, Lincoln, Bonhoeffer, Jesus — we killed these people for being *themselves*.

You can't hide the authentic life. It unsettles things. Provokes things. You might quit your job. Move. Stop hating someone. Start giving things away, such as your time, your money, your entitlement . . . your life.

You will laugh more. You will certainly suffer more, and because of that, suffer less. Things will be unfamiliar, and because of that, sometimes fearful. But you will make friends with your fear and, because of that, not be afraid of your fear.

The authentic life is sometimes a holy terror, because often it begins by revealing what is embarrassingly inauthentic. Don't give up. One of the surest signs that we have begun the journey of authentic living is found in the earnest confession, "This ain't it."

You'll get used to it.

You don't need a paintbrush to be an artist

Art is such a mystery. Some people simply must interpret and claim their human experience through some artistic medium. They paint. They draw. They sing. They write. They create.

The rest of us are blessed by the artist's endeavor because, if it is art, we find our own human story in the artist's work. A paradox: Great art is always uniquely personal to the artist, yet its connection to the wider world is universal. Artists often wonder if they are exhibitionists. But it is not the artist we are staring at. It is ourselves.

If you are an artist in any medium, then you've heard it before. Friends or strangers have leaned over your sketch, your painting, listened to your song or admired your craft, shook their head and said, "I'm just not very artistic." For most people, the world is neatly divided into "artists" and "not-artists."

If you want to provoke anxiety in the average person, ask him to draw a picture in front of his peers. You can graduate from anxiety to panic by asking that same person to prepare and give a public speech. For sheer terror, ask him to sing and dance in front of an audience. Most of us are glad to have artists around because that significantly reduces the chances that anyone might ask us to express ourselves artistically.

Don't get me wrong. I'm not one of those folks who says that everyone could be an artist if he or she really tried. It's not true, at least not in the classic sense of the word "artist." I have a friend, for example, whose brain can't hear him sing. I know this because, if my friend's brain could hear my friend sing, my friend would immediately stop singing. He loves me that much.

But there's another, lesser-known use of the word "art." We English-speaking folks borrowed the word "politic" from the ancient Greeks. Politic means "the art of human relationship." Today the word "politic" is used mostly as a pejorative. When a relationship is described as "political," we usually mean that someone is dishonestly manipulating us or others. But this definition is an unfortunate devolution of language. All relationships have politics, and good politics make for good relationships. Marriage requires a careful, intentional politic. My politics with my moody middle-schooler are sometimes like Death Chess Match. On Mother's Day, how many of you carefully shape the politic of your relationship with your mother?

Great relationship is great art. It is a uniquely personal expression of self, opening up a universal window through which others see a glimpse of their own human hope. If we think about relationship as a legitimate artistic medium, then, yes, I would say that everyone can be an artist. Everyone should be.

So, if you never choose to pursue a traditional artistic endeavor

— if you never dip a paint brush, or sculpt a stone, or write a poem, or compose a song, or design software, or rebut the Theory of Relativity — there remains one artistic medium available and demanded of everyone: Have a relationship.

Make a commitment to something or, better yet, to someone. Because, finally, all art (from statue to sonnet to watercolor) is a living echo and reflection of human relationship — with lovers, friends, parents, children, Earth, cosmos, ideals, Source, Being. With God. In committed relationship, people create and re-create themselves and each other. Meaning emerges.

Be reminded that there are very few prodigies working in the medium of relationship. The most important factor in the occasional masterpiece is that we have kept at it.

Respect a person's right to be closed

One of my favorite insecurities is my fear of being perceived as glib. Truth is, my preferred persona is glib. When it works for me, it comes off as casual, easy, nonchalant. Not stiff. It puts people at ease. When it doesn't work, it comes off as unthinking, unreflecting, cocky. The inability to take things seriously.

As with so many personality traits, it is at once a celebration of my true nature (I'm not stiff) *and* a defense. I am in fact SO serious about things such as meaning and truth and beauty that it overwhelms me sometimes. Glib is my way of creating some comforting distance between myself and my passions.

But glib is a therapeutic strategy, too.

"I suppose you want to know about my past," says the man during his first session, all obedient and serious and deferent.

"Nope," I say, all chipper and friendly and glib.

This surprises him. Confuses him. Permanently changes our relationship, which is only about seven minutes old.

"Really," he says.

"Really," I say. "I don't *want* to know anything . . . except whatever it is you came here to say. Do you want to talk about your past? Do you need to?"

He breaks eye contact and falls into himself. Silence. This is good. Here but a few minutes and already he's thinking in new ways. I'm glad for him.

One of my favorite ways to respect people is to respect their right to be closed. Sometimes this entails reminding people they have that right, which was the case with my response to this man. The way he posed his inquiry abdicates too much power to me. I'm not idly curious. I'm not a voyeur. Therapy isn't about what I want to know about you. It's about what *you'd* like to know about you.

To be truly open, one must have the capacity to be truly closed. Think about it.

There's a name for people who CAN'T be closed, for people who must always be cranked wide open for the whole world to see: exhibitionist. And opening one's raincoat at the train station to expose nakedness is only one kind of exhibitionism. Others of us cannot *not* whip open the raincoat around our hearts, our thoughts, our every desire, our sufferings.

It isn't healthy.

A friend wants to know if I'd like to go to Black's Beach in San Diego. Nude beach. Whole families go there to splash in the waves and play paddle ball on the beach . . . naked. I tell him "no" without hesitation.

Yeah, yeah, I get that Americans are all hung up about sex and nudity. I know about other cultures where it's "no big deal." But none of that is my point. My concern is that an eleven-year-old girl, for example, raised from birth in the subculture of nudism, might not know she has permission to be closed. And, developmentally, this is exactly what she should be learning right now.

It's been fun to raise boys. Boys frolic naked a lot. Then suddenly they don't. My five-year-old now says, "It's okay for you to come in, Pop, but not girls, because we need privacy from girls."

I help him brush his teeth, and I reach absent-mindedly to put counter-pressure on the nape of his neck. Done it a thousand times. But this time he jerks away indignantly and says, "I'm in charge of my own body!"

He is quoting his preschool teacher. I like it. And I respect it. And I apologize for my too-familiar entitlement to touch his body. We renegotiate respect.

Soon, he won't merely close the bathroom door, but I'll hear the "tink" of the passage lock. And soon enough he'll close his bedroom door more often. He'll step outside to talk to his friends on the phone. He'll not tell me about every crush on every girl. He'll not disclose his every fear and insecurity, or his every hope and dream. He'll be a separate person.

This is all good and right and healthy.

Exhibitionism is a way to control and manipulate. The ability to remain closed makes true intimacy possible. It is respectful to self and others.

"Would you like this door open or closed?" asks my colleague as she leaves my office.

"You can leave it open," I say. But how very flattering of her to ask.

Giving someone permission to be closed is often the very thing that makes it more likely for them to open.

Throw out that self-improvement to-do list

My friend buys me a book about my Enneagram Type. The Enneagram is an ancient theory observing nine variations of human personality type. (Check out *The Enneagram* by Helen Palmer or *Personality Types* by Don Richard Riso.)

In the first chapter heading, I'm described as romantic, melancholic, a dramatist. "You need to practice contemplative spiritual disciplines," my friend says.

"Yeah," I reply, "and you need to get drunk more often." We both laugh out loud.

Please don't get the idea that I was rebuffing my friend's descriptions of me, or his prescriptions regarding my self-improvement. To the contrary, my Enneagram Type is stone-cold accurate, and my friend is correct that my life could well be deepened and improved were I to spend more time in silence, in contemplation, in meditation, etc.

My life also would be improved were I to eat more broccoli and fewer Dairy Queen Oreo Blizzards. I also should watch less TV and pay more attention to my children. I could be a more cheerful help-mate to my friends. I need to improve my organizational skills and attention to detail. I should call my mother more often. I should . . . I could . . . Hope you've got some time on your hands, because it's a long list.

Ah, The List. Everybody's got a list. On the list are all the ways we could be better. Do better. Be more. And I used to think that perpetually rehearsing and updating my list was the mark of serious spirituality and deepening moral character. Not anymore. Today I think of that impulse as an oppression, an impedance to creative living. I no longer need to ground each day in the reality of The List. My life today is grounded in a deeper reality. A miracle, actually. To whit, I'm surrounded and upheld by people who, astonishingly enough, love me DESPITE what is on my List. It's outrageous.

Socrates said "the unexamined life is not worth living." Socrates is absolutely right and oh so wrong. Let's take those things one at a time:

Socrates is right. To live well, we must have some capacity to know ourselves. Otherwise, we are doomed to live unconsciously. I'm always intrigued when I meet people with a passionate preference for oblivion — people who seemingly are never curious about their own motives, people with no apparent ability or perhaps willingness to perceive themselves being perceived. How many times have you listened to a public speaker, preacher, or lecturer and thought, "Wow, Speaker, if you could see and feel what I was seeing and feeling in this audience, you'd stop talking and sit down."

On the other hand, Socrates is wrong. Neither is the perpetually and obsessively examined life worth living. There's a line between healthy self-awareness and paralyzing self-consciousness. The attributes of ANY personality have both positive and negative dimensions.

Of course I'm dramatic. I like it. I think life is pregnant with drama, and I enjoy the rush. Of course, being dramatic regularly leaves me unsettled and emotionally fragmented. Of course, my presence fatigues some folks who naturally prefer a more sensible and intro-verted and measured way of life. Good for them. And good for me. I don't raise my brow at them and say, "Geez, you're kinda dull and boring and constrained and uptight . . . you should consider bungee jumping or falling in love or a vacation at a nude beach." Nope — I assume they are living exactly as they like to live. And they can bet I'm doing that, too.

What REALLY needs to be fixed in us? I'm thinking more and more that the answer is our obsession with needing to be fixed. Try giving up The List for one week. If you don't behave any better, or any worse, then ask yourself why you keep The List at all.

The goal is a riddle: Know yourself. Then stop thinking about yourself.

Choosing emotional growth is a hero's journey

Many people who present themselves for therapy are more or less chagrined to have come at all. They presuppose that something is wrong with them. They understand their very presence in therapy to be a confession of reprehensible weakness, brokenness, some sort of dereliction for which they should feel a sense of shame and embar-rassment. "I don't know why I/we can't figure this out by ourselves," they'll say with no small degree of self-loathing.

Something is wrong with us. That's why we're in therapy. This is not just a common individual prejudice; that same prejudice lives collectively, too, in our culture.

I once was required to fill out a background check and histori-cal questionnaire for employment. The form included the question, "Have you ever been treated for a mental illness or mental disorder?" I checked the box that said "no." Later on that same form, I disclosed that I once participated in depth psychotherapy — weekly, for three years and eight months, to be precise. (I had a lot to talk about.) The supervisor accused me in writing of being less than honest on the form. How could I have been in depth psychotherapy for so long but still check "no" on the question about mental illness or mental disorder? Or so the supervisor reasoned.

I wrote back to say that such conclusions were worse than flawed. The conclusions were nothing more than the regurgitation of a deep-seated cultural bias. To whit: If you're in therapy, something must be wrong with you. The accusation was saying a lot more about the supervisor than about me, I said. Never got a reply.

For my way of thinking, it's rarely what's wrong with people that brings them to therapy. Rather, they are drawn to therapy because of what's *right* within them. What's right within them is the universal human instinct for wholeness.

When a human being is living in willful blindness, unconscious self-deception, or even a psychotic state — that would sooner or later be all of us — that human being will tend to develop symptoms. Could be anything. Might be the estrangement of an important relationship. Might be an inexplicable inability to manage moods and emotions. Might be a compulsive behavior — drugs, alcohol, gambling, food, sex, or bad religion. Might be depression. Might be violence to self or others. What we don't work out, we tend to act out. Whatever we won't face in ourselves tends to show up in the people and circumstances around us. It's cosmic law.

What's right about people who come to therapy is their pervasive hunch, more or less conscious, that this ain't it. This is not the life they want. Something is incomplete. Something is false. Not entirely authentic. There's got to be more. What brings them to therapy is their own integrity, combined with courage, humility, and healthy self-interest. These are good things.

Yeah, people come to talk about marriage, relationships, sex, child-rearing, the management of moods and emotions, sex, trauma present and past, addictions and other destructive behavior, and sometimes sex. People come to talk about grief, guilt, and loss. But you already suspected all that, didn't you?

I'm saying that behind the common symptoms and presenting issues of modern clients, I often tell myself that there is another journey at once ordinary and profound. It is the universal human journey of a developing identity. It is the search for meaning, for if we find meaning there is no agony or ecstasy that we cannot endure.

The restlessness and suffering in the human heart is often the result of a war inside us between our twisted fondness for inertia and the heroic hunger for movement and growth.

Every day we choose.

We mean exactly what we say and do

Here's my favorite therapy joke:

> *Woman goes to her psychoanalyst and says, "Doctor, doctor — remember how you have been asking me to pay attention to Freudian slips? Well, I'm real excited because I think I might have finally caught myself in a Freudian slip!"*
>
> *Doctor says, "Good, good! Terrific! Tell me about it."*
>
> *Woman says, "Well, the other morning I sat down for breakfast. My husband was sitting across from me, reading the paper. I meant to say, 'Please pass me the cinnamon rolls,' and instead I said, 'You son of a bitch, you ruined my life.'"*

I hate what I'm about to say. I hate that it's true. I would rather it not be true. But it is true, so here goes:

People tend to say exactly what they mean. People tend to do exactly the thing they most want to do.

Sigmund Freud said a lot of things in his intellectual career. Some of his ideas have been assailed, critiqued, even discredited. But here's my favorite Sigmund Freud quote: "The consequences of our actions tend to reveal our motives." Yep. It's unassailable. Inarguable. Disquieting. Absolutely true.

Consider the way married people reconcile after a fight:

> *Spouse 1: "I'm sorry, honey. I didn't mean to hurt you."*
>
> *Spouse 2: "Oh, that's okay."*
>
> *(Smooch, hug, etc.)*

But it's not the truth. It's more of a cultural ceremony. I'm not even saying there is anything wrong with the ceremony. I'm just noticing that if we waved a Freudian wand over the couple, the dialogue would be different:

> *Spouse 1: "I need to apologize — not just for hurting you, but*

for wanting to hurt you. You see, I'm an expert at hurting you.
Nobody's better. I've known you for a long time, and I know just
how to hurt you. Tone, pace, word choice, volume — I'm the
master. And in that exact moment, the thing I most wanted to do
was hurt you. So I did.

    Spouse 2: "Yikes."

People tend to say exactly what they mean. People tend to do exactly the thing they most want to do.

Seen from the perspective of my religious life, I would say it this way: I wish I could sin accidentally more often. You know — oops. Sorry. Accidentally lusted after my dental hygienist. Stumbled into a pile of gossip there. Has it really been six months since I went to the gym? Hmm. Inertia. What a mystery. Stuff happens. My bad.

But I don't sin accidentally very often. I look a cheap and inferior choice for living right in the eye and say "Yippee . . . you're coming with me!"

I don't make that many mistakes. I make choices. Sometimes the choices are swift, conscious, and decisive. But many times I make choices in passive, imperceptible increments — an obscure decision here, a minor denial there, a juggling of laudable aspirations with too-human illusions. When the day of reckoning comes, I'm wont to feign surprise, but don't buy it. I have a lifetime membership in Non-Innocents of America.

You?

Seems strange to say it, but if I know that I'm miserable, and I know that I'm not innocent, then I'm back in charge. Change is possible.

People tend to say exactly what they mean. People tend to do exactly the thing they most want to do.

Your friends and enemies are right about you

A parable: "A man is free to choose his friends and his enemies. Once having made the choice, he must live with the consequences. And so must his friends. And so must his enemies."

Have you noticed that your friends and enemies are both right about you?

My colleague tells me I'm "a real showmen," and I don't think she's being complimentary. Nope — it's a first-class indictment. She says I "have a real need to be in the center of things." This explains why I can't be trusted and why I'm probably phonier than a three-dollar bill. If you could see into this woman's eyes, you'd see she believes herself to possess special insight about me. She *knows*. She encourages me to seek therapy.

A few days later, another colleague calls to ask me to participate in a special project. "Steven," he says, "I need you to come here and really turn it on. We need your energy — someone who won't be boring and who can gather us together to focus on some new ways of thinking and doing."

He doesn't understand why my response to his request is to laugh out loud.

I tell him that another colleague had, just a few days earlier, observed the exact same attributes of my personality but had drawn a starkly different conclusion. I inform him that he'd better watch out, that I had recently learned about this overwhelming need I had to be in the center of things.

"I don't know — or care — if you need to be in the center of things, Steven," he said. "I just know that your personality frequently *puts* you in the center of things. The only way you could avoid that would be to deny who you are . . . to be a fraud . . . to pretend to be somebody else."

Our friends and enemies are both right. You think "enemies" is too strong? Maybe it's enough to simply call them not-friends. But the point remains they both are accurate in their observations about us. They are looking at the same thing. The same person. So, if they are looking at the same thing and seeing the same thing accurately, why is one a friend and the other not?

A not-friend observes your temperament, your gifts, your foibles, your idiosyncrasies, your absurd habits, immaturities, and character flaws, and moves immediately to build narratives (that is, to spin a yarn) about how unique and remarkable are your failures and negative impact upon the world. To the not-friend, you are a special case, deserving of particular sanctions and editorial critique. Maybe you deserve to be shunned, ostracized, punished, or even attacked. At the very least, you need to be corrected.

Your friend, on the other hand, sees those exact same things — mind you, precisely the same data — shrugs and says, "Oh, that's just [your name here]." For some mysterious reason, your friend doesn't have the same need to advance the negative narrative. To a friend, you personality is neither here nor there. It's just you.

Worst case, if your behavior was to become openly disrespectful or otherwise unbearable, your friend would pull you aside, ask you what in blue blazes is going on, and would you kindly knock it off. But it wouldn't be a big deal. It would not be an indictment, *ad hominem*.

Remind me to spend more time with my friends.

Making distinctions is a natural way of forming bonds

My friend argues with me when she hears me make distinctions between styles and types of human relationships. She says my worldview is analogous to the landmark case *Brown vs. Board of Education*. This famous case obviated once and for all the idea of "separate but equal." This case decoded "separate but equal" and exposed its true and malicious meaning: "I very much *want* to stay separate because I think you are anything *but* equal to me."

My friend makes me think a long time. Then it hits me. I didn't say "separate but equal." I don't believe in "separate but equal." What I said was "distinct and maybe or maybe not equal."

My friend worries about me making distinctions, because people have the bad habit of using distinctions as justification for denigrating one another. I understand completely. My friend makes an accurate historical observation about human nature. But the solution for that evil is not to stop making distinctions. Ignoring distinctions only gives rise to other evils.

We have a duty to hone a keen discernment with which we then must make important and necessary distinctions. Once we make a distinction, we again employ our discernment to ascertain whether things are equal. Perhaps they are equal. Perhaps they are not. Or perhaps they are so different as to make irrelevant a value comparison.

Modern culture too often advances the strange idea that intimacy, pluralism, and diversity happen when we stop making distinctions. Wrong. Just the opposite. Healthy culture — not to mention all healthy relationship — encourages us to acknowledge and respect differences. Modern psychology calls this process "individuation." A Buddhist parable reminds us: "This is not that."

A man is not a woman.

A mother is not a father.

My Honda Accord is not an SUV (a lesson I learned painfully on our last camping trip).

A Christian is not a Buddhist, nor is a Buddhist a Jew.

Cohabitation is not marriage.

I am not a nineteen-year-old college basketball player (and I have the doctor bills to prove it).

Pepsi isn't Coke.

A homosexual is not a heterosexual.

The Beatles are not Britney Spears (do ya think?).

Las Vegas is not Disneyland.

A wife is not her husband, nor a husband his wife.

A child is not an adult.

When a real dog barks, it never makes the sound "yip." (Okay, that's more a prejudice than a distinction).

Healthy relationships make and maintain vital distinctions. If I am to enjoy intimacy, pluralism, and diversity — with a woman, my family, my neighborhood, other cultures — then I must identify and honor the "holy otherness" of others.

It happens that the drummer in my band is a black man. At our last recording session I was unhappy with a drum track on a particular song. We bounced some ideas back and forth, and then he said it: "So, is this just straight white rock?" I blushed, but I wasn't offended. He didn't denigrate me. He wasn't even trying to be funny. He was simply cutting to the chase, articulating a candid distinction between rhythm styles practiced and preferred by my ear and rhythm styles practiced and preferred by his ear. I chuckled and said, "Exactly — straight white rock." He left the drum kit throbbing. I loved it and I told him so. He just rolled his eyes.

I'm a white folk-rock songwriter. My drummer is black and tours with the Pointer Sisters. I am not him. He is not me. We're different. We are both quite clear on these points. And precisely because we make these distinctions, an intimate and creative collegiality opens like a flower between us.

Our names are precious — and powerful

My name is Steven. It's Greek (*stavros* = "crown"), though I'm mostly Saxon with a little tweener of McDaniel Scot thrown in for good measure.

Names matter. Names have power. Names are big medicine. By the time we're in preschool, we know there is no more efficient and sure method for degrading people than by degrading their names. Conversely, there are few more efficient and sure methods for conveying respect than to inquire after a person's name — to use it, to remember it, to pronounce it correctly.

We live in a world of instant nicknames and presumed familiarities. In this culture of instant intimacy, we afford ourselves the presumption of inventing nicknames and endearments for people we barely know. We tell ourselves we're being friendly and warm and hospitable when we do this, but I wonder.

"What's your name?" the car salesman asks.

"Steven," I answer.

"Hey, Steeverino!" the salesman exclaims.

"Close, but it's pronounced Stee-vuhn, with the accent on the first syllable," I say.

Steeverino is more like the name of a dry cleaner, or a car wash, or the name of a process for removing fabric stains. *Don't worry, ma'am; we'll just run this through the Steeverino and it should be fine.*

"What's your name?" people ask.

"Steven," I answer.

"Steve, it's nice to meet you," they say.

And it's all I can do not to interrupt right then and there and say, "Pardon me, but, if you were just gonna make up a name for me anyway, why'd you ask? I mean, why didn't you just say, 'Hello, Mitch' or 'Hello, Barbara'?"

"Hi, Steve," people greet me.

"Just curious," I want to say, "but of all the arbitrary places to suddenly stop saying my name, why'd you pick between the e and the n? I mean, why didn't you say Stev, or Ste, or St, or Ssssss?"

Names matter. There's no such thing as "just a name." Names don't merely represent identity; names participate in our identity. In some sense, names contain our identity. Which is why people sometimes change their names. When our identity moves through a time of profound transformation, sometimes our old name no longer fits. I've known people who have completed a rigorous course of psychotherapy and then punctuated that work by changing their name. Now they are someone else.

It happens in religion, too. Both the Hebrew and Christian scriptures are replete with folks who, once they meet God, are so transformed that their old names can no longer contain their new identity. Abram becomes Abraham. Sarai becomes Sarah. Simon becomes Peter. Saul becomes Paul. Islam, too. Lew Alcindor was a great college basketball player. But it's Kareem Abdul-Jabbar who owns the professional scoring record. Two different names. Two different men.

If you tell me your name, you surrender some degree of power to me. With that power I can actually make you physically turn around. All I have to do is walk up behind you and call your name.

If you know my name, but I don't know yours, you will have a kind of power over me, which, where I come from, is a breech of decorum. The ever-polite English would say it this way: "Sir, you have me at a disadvantage." Translation: "Hey, mind your manners! Introduce yourself before you go on jabbering at me like we're old friends! It's disrespectful to bandy my name about while you remain disguised in anonymity."

When I hear the name "Steve," I'm not insulted. I don't get my feelings hurt. I won't even move to correct you. But in my heart, I will quietly register the fact that you don't know me. And if you intend to hang around in my space for any length of time, it is my hope that you would want to know me. To respect me.

Truth is, "Steve" is the name of a boy I once was. Embarrassingly enough, I was mostly that boy well into my thirties. Then life, love, fatherhood, and other such realities dragged me off and grew me up. Steve is the boy. Steven is the man — both the man I am and the one I hope to become.

"Do you prefer Steve or Steven?" asks my new colleague.

"Steven," I say. "And thanks for asking."

Self-consciousness is an impediment to our happiest moments

It's the number one social phobia on every survey. Strikes terror in the hearts of most Americans. Provokes parasympathetic sweats. People would sooner cut off their own thumbs.

The fear of public speaking.

Public speaking can and regularly does make otherwise intelligent people feel stupid. Sometimes sound stupid. But it's not about intelligence. It's about fear, and the painful self-consciousness that fear provokes.

Self-consciousness is not the same as self-awareness. Self-awareness is a good thing. Self-consciousness is the paralysis of self that comes when all we can do is notice ourselves being noticed . . . see ourselves being seen.

It's something like the worst attack of claustrophobia combined with having a stroke. Your tongue becomes strangely thick. Your throat compressed. Your jaw no longer entirely in your command. Your arm and hand movements have all the sincerity of a badly played marionette.

People routinely quit great jobs or refuse to apply for great jobs that require public speaking and public presentations.

I am frequently surprised by the prevalence of this social phobia, because, well, I never met a microphone I didn't like. Public speaking is fun for me, like bungee-jumping is fun for other people (also known as crazy people). Sometimes I think the bigger the audience and the less time I have to prepare, the better. There's something inside of me that just knows what to do.

Do I get nervous? Sure. But for some reason the adrenaline rush is part of what's fun for me. Makes me focused, alert, and ready.

My work includes bopping around the country for a variety of teaching, training, after lunch/dinner public speaking invitations. Yet, just about the time I start feeling smug about my public speaking prowess, it occurs to me that they might just be paying me to show up and talk so they don't have to. Like that kid on that old cereal commercial. "Hey, Mikey! He'll eat anything!"

But lest you think I'm invulnerable to paralyzing self-consciousness, you should see me at Gilley's trying to dance. Or later, after a sufficient number of my friends made fun of me, when I took lessons at Dance Charisma.

It's so bizarre. I was once a fair athlete. Basketball player. I could move fluidly and effortless across the court. Never had a conscious thought about jumping, running, crossover dribbling, head fakes. Just did it. So why, when I stand face to face with a woman who'd like to strut her stuff to Toby Keith, do I become a world-class geek? Suddenly it's like being behind the wheel of a car I've never driven. I'm rigid and stiff and . . . painfully self-conscious. Every movement is a careful thought. Which adds up to being a bad dancer.

Remember the episode of *Happy Days* when Fonzie tried to be the lead singer of a rock band? The always "together" hipster suddenly became a puddle of self-doubt, fear, and nausea. Remember the episode of *Friends* when Chandler is trying to pose for a wedding engagement photograph? The otherwise suave and ever-witty fiancée is frozen by the camera lens and succeeds only in doing facial caricatures of himself.

Everybody has some setting in which they experience unhappy and frustrating self-consciousness. Art forms are a frequent culprit: public speaking, singing, dancing, drawing, humor. Courtship and falling in love can render us incapable of constructing simple sentences. Some people become very self-conscious in the company of infants and toddlers. They hold them with all the naturalness and comfort they might hold, say, a bucket of dung. Or a time bomb.

Which brings me to the colloquialism "to lose oneself." You'll hear a great screen performance described as ". . . the actor just lost himself in that role." You'll hear a basketball player on a shooting hot streak described as "unconscious." We lose ourselves in some activity or work or relationship when we stop noticing ourselves and stop noticing ourselves being noticed. We are fully present to the experience.

It is in such moments that human beings are the most creative. The most likeable. Make the fewest mistakes. At once the most brilliant and the most humble. They are supremely happy.

So why don't we do it more often? How do we learn to lose ourselves and simply flow with the joy of being human?

I don't know. Really. When those moments come, it's like the golden light that showers the Sword in the Stone before young Arthur pulls it free.

Suddenly, you just *can*.

Celebrating middle age with gratitude and snobbery

Fifty is coming at me like a train. Scheduled arrival: July 5, 2007.

The strangest part is not my terror of physical decline. Naw — I can live with the irony that I can still whup my fifteen-year-old in one-on-one basketball . . . just before I collapse with a groin pull.

Lucky for my son, though, to have the opportunity to get to know his dad better. He got a nice glimpse of me the once-competent basketball player, and then a nice preview of me proto-geezer, grimacing and writhing on the gym floor, gripping my crotch.

His dad's a multidimensional guy.

Neither is the strangest part of turning fifty my terror of realizing I'm nearly invisible now at nightclubs and bars. Well, there was this one girl-woman who stopped in front of my bar stool recently to dance seductively in front of me. Sure enough, up popped the Hubba-hubba Window on my brain monitor: "Hey, I recall that you're attracted to female homo sapien primates with those eyes and that hair and a body shaped like that."

Unfortunately, then she began to speak. I think she was telling me about all that she'd had to drink. I think. You've heard of a spam blocker for computers? Well, somewhere along the way I uploaded my brain with Stupid Drunk Blocker. The Hubba-hubba Window closed without a fight.

No, the strangest part of fifty is the overwhelming sense I have of *starting all over*. Like everything before this was just some protracted rehearsal. Like maybe I just read about some guy in his teens, twenties, thirties and forties. Like what I have described heretofore as my greatest joys and my greatest sufferings will both pale when compared with what lies ahead.

Like I don't know anything. At all.

I used to have this List of Certainties. One column was marked "Things I know about myself that are meritorious and just all-around pretty cool." Another column was marked "Gross character flaws that I'd change immediately if I had an ounce of character." As I head for fifty, I'm aware that I'm abandoning both lists. I'm not at all sure either is very accurate; and even when accurate, not particularly relevant.

I just know that some things about being me are really fun for me. Other things make me wonder why I have any friends at all.

The strangest part of turning fifty is noticing the two new columns that are dominating my List of Certainties: gratitude and snobbery. You wouldn't think those two things would be related, but they are. The more I'm aware of my gratitude, the more surgically selective I become regarding how I spend my time, and who I spend it with.

Life is stunningly brief, and when you "get" that, gratitude and snobbery seem the only logical response.

I no longer feel obligated to finish a bad book.

I don't spend time with mean people, or with people who need me to feel bad about myself, even if I'm related to them.

I terminate poisonous relationships. Just like that.

I trust myself to know the difference between true art and when

I'm being jacked around by a poser.

I will not allow myself to be bored. Boredom is a sin.

I'm willing to suffer for a profound value, but I'm no longer willing to suffer just so willful stupidity or corruption can continue in blithe oblivion. I either speak up, or go do something else.

This coming Thursday, I shall practice gratitude. I will reflect on the absolutely absurd, ridiculously long list of joys and blessings in my life for which I can take no credit whatsoever. I'll also practice snobbery, because I won't be eating Thanksgiving dinner with people who are ambivalent about me. I eat with people who both know me and love me. They're nice to me. Fun to be with.

And if they overcook the turkey, I'll concentrate on the wine and the side dishes.

Life is too short to eat dry turkey breast.

Real courage is doing what has to be done

I find myself at Joshua Tree National Monument in California. About three stories off the ground.

My cheek is pressed like a desperate lover against the cool of the sandstone. My fingers grip a fissure in the rock face. My right foot crowds two of my five toes into a hole a little bigger than a golf ball. My left foot, pointed ninety degrees to the right, is ironically the most secure part of my body, grounded solidly on an actual, discernable ledge.

I'm wearing these weird rubber Spider-Man shoes. Around my pelvis is a harness that gives new meaning to the phrase "gird your loins." My loins are so well-girded, I could join the local boys choir. A rope proceeds out of the harness and goes up — and up and up . . . and then back down where it rests in the hands of my instructor. The same place my life rests. He says he'll be keeping slack in the rope so I can have the experience of really climbing this vertical rock face by myself. How generous of him.

I'm scared. I don't mean a little nervous. I'm terrified. Fear hammers in my chest. My breath is panicky. Tears come to my eyes, despite my efforts to erase them with self-loathing. Geez. I'm weeping.

The instructor says there is a small hand-hold above and to the right, that if I place my grip there, I can push off from my left foot and make progress. I say "Roger, that," and remain motionless. The fear is physical. A compression gravity. My arms and legs ignore my will, like they belong to someone else.

Indeed, my appendages belong to my fear.

It's not like I'm content, safe and secure where I am. I hate where I am. I'm afraid to stay. I'm afraid to move. But the trifecta of my fear is that I am most afraid to go backward, to say, "Stop, quit, let me down." This is my worst nightmare of all. Giving up. Quitting. It would be too much like a . . .

. . . stillbirth. In my mind I see my wife in labor with our first child. I see the pain and uncertainty in her eyes. "I don't know if I can do this," she says at one point. "Yes, you can," I say, meaning to encourage but immediately thinking what a stupid thing to say. It's not like she can change her mind. The window for decision making closed nine months ago, right after I kissed her. Nothing to do now but be as scared as you need to be and do it anyway.

Feels like I'm being born on this rock climb. Feels like I'm pregnant with myself, in labor with me. I don't know if I can do this. It wasn't even my idea. I never, ever of my own accord would have said to my wife, "Hey, let's face abject fear and risk suffering and death by learning how to rock climb." Nope — we just happen to love this couple who are nuts about this sport and we made the mistake of bringing them camping with us. Like most experiences that stretch our limits, this experience is a consequence of my vulnerability to relationship. I didn't choose it. The relationship challenged it in me.

If those glib folks on the ground only knew just how perfectly this moment was reflecting my life. I have some growing to do. Long, long overdue growing. I'm scared beyond words. I don't know if I can do the growing, or really even how to do it. I would never have chosen it, or even particularly thought it was necessary. But there's this relationship in my life to which I am intensely vulnerable. The relationship is stuck. If I do nothing, the relationship will die. If I quit, I will never be born.

There's really no choice but forward — on this rock or in my relationship. With a primordial bellow echoing across the national park I evict my left foot from its false security and lift myself toward a place I've never been and don't know how to get to. I don't know who I'll be when I get there, because getting there is changing me.

I've never met this person who's being born. Hope I like him.

Courage never feels like courage. Courage is never the absence of fear. Real courage is the willingness to feel debilitating fear, and then doing what needs to be done anyway. If you wait to feel confident and courageous, you'll never be born.

Authenticity matters in music and other parts of life

I'm looking down the barrel of a five-hour drive, but I'm armed with the new CD *Bitter Suite Swan Song* from the pop band Poppermost. Never heard of Poppermost? Well then, give yourself a right smack on the forehead and come with me.

Poppermost is the songwriting duo Alex Oliver and Roy Al Rendahl. I have followed and enjoyed their career for a few years now, but *Bitter Suite* is like nothing they have ever done. I listen to it three times during my five-hour drive, and I keep shaking my head and smiling. Melody. Relentless melody that just takes you apart. Vocal harmony to send shivers down your back. Lyrics that combine a disarming innocence with ruthless candor.

My favorite track is "Down," a song that, without irony, lets us remember the way love draws us like a moth to the flame, illuminating everything, then tearing us limb from limb:

> *Love can be as trivial just like a matchbox*
> *Left beside somebody's birthday cake*
> *And love can pierce the soul just like an arrow*
> *If it feels at odds with your mistakes*

I opened my e-mail this morning to find yet another story about Britney Spears. This time she's been busted for lip synching. The fans boo. Actually, the only thing that surprises me about the story is that there remains any appreciable number of "music fans" in America who understand such things ought to be booed.

Unfortunately for her, Britney has become, for me, an icon of sorts, and not the sort of icon you'd want to be. She represents for me all that is false and empty about the modern music industry. She's not a musician. She's not a writer. Her singing voice, reasonably ordinary to begin with, is poured through multiple filters and compressors. Maybe it's a person. But maybe it's an android escaped from a Stanley Kubrick film.

Britney herself brought two special gifts to the table to place before the gods of entertainment whimsy in America. She can dance. Oh my she can dance. The bulk of her training as a child was in gymnastics and dance. And she has a compelling navel.

Mostly I'm just sad for her.

I'm going on record right now: You'll never see "Britney Unplugged" on VH1, and fifty years from now, nostalgic, aging music fans will not be buying boxed set anthologies of Britney Spears. Never gonna happen.

Actually, I blame the soulless state of the modern music industry on The Monkees. That's where it all began. In the wake of the peerless Beatles, the British Invasion sent great pop act after great pop act to America. ABC and Colgem Records had a brainchild: Why wait for the emergence of a great American band when we can invent one? The casting call yielded Mike, Davey, Peter, and Mickey. They hired stud songwriters such as Carol King and Neil Diamond. Ripped off the format from the movie *Hard Day's Night*. One audience of eager Monkee fans couldn't wait, so they booed the warm-up act off the stage. Guy named Jimi Hendrix.

If you were part of that audience, I urge you to go to rock 'n' roll confession and clear your conscience.

Used to be the fundamental job of a disc jockey was *not* to cue records and make happy talk, but to *listen* to listeners. They spent off-air time combing coffeehouses, bars, street corners, small theaters, international news services, always on the look-out for brilliance, talent, poetry. They looked for great songwriters.

Today, disc jockeys play what they are told to play. Guys in suits gather in board rooms and decide what you and I are going to like next. If Bob Dylan was nineteen today, sitting on a bar stool in a Minnesota coffeehouse with his hardly above-average guitar skills, using that wretched-but-real voice of his to launch lyrics that don't happen but once every one hundred years or so . . .

. . . we'd never know. Because he'd never stand a chance.

The reason you've never heard of Poppermost is because the band isn't famous. I only know about the band because I hang out in bars on open mic nights and listen to gutsy, courageous, sometimes gifted, sometimes not-so-gifted nobodies (like me) play and sing original music in smoky rooms for an audience of mostly other writers.

I listen to Alex and Roy not just because I like them, but because they are real. Authentic. Loaded with talent. Their craft matters to them. They risk themselves.

I don't buy Britney Spears records for the same reason I will never buy an artificial Christmas tree.

Spiritual Matters

THERE ARE AT LEAST A HANDFUL OF THINGS UNIQUE AND PECULIAR TO THE *HOMO SAPIEN* ANIMAL.

We laugh and cry. Most people are convinced that higher mammals experience emotions or feelings, but we're the only ones who express significant emotion with a spontaneous, biological response involving tear ducts, lungs, and the rhythmic movement of the diaphragm. In fact, if you think about it, the physiology of laughing and crying is virtually identical. One feels lousy. The other feels good. Both create endorphins and a sense of greater calm.

We require and are compelled to create symbols and art. I get that you can teach gorillas and chimpanzees to use American Sign Language. But only human beings feel the need to paint on cave walls and canvasses and church ceilings. Only human beings sculpt and exchange wedding rings. No chimpanzee, after consummating a courtship, ever said, "Was it good for you?"

We talk. That is, we use language. Other animals communicate, yes, but they don't talk. There is a difference. This is actually a subset of the above discussion of symbols, since it is the nature of language to be symbolic.

All animals exist, but it seems that human beings *know* they exist. Perhaps dolphins and humpbacks and my Aussie shepherd Kelly have some sentient understanding that they exist, but it not the same as a human understanding. See, the primary way we know we exist is because we also know that someday we'll cease to exist. That is, we know we're going to die. And this bothers us. Really bothers us. Consciously or unconsciously.

It's called existential anxiety. No other life form appears to manifest it. Wildebeests can exhibit anxiety, distress, even something like fear when wild dogs come to eat them alive. But this is instinctual — not philosophical. African elephants at, say, age fifty-three, show no evidence of brooding, "Gee, where did the time go? I promised myself I'd see Kenya before I died."

No other animals contemplate whether they have made a good and proper use of their time on Earth.

And lastly is the universal human need to transcend. Human beings can't stop reaching beyond their own physical environment, their finite forms, their experience, even their own consciousness.

I'm not joking: Mind-altering substances show up early in human history. Beer shows up in the Middle East around the fourth or fifth millennium B.C.E., and many archaeologists believe earlier than that in Africa. Wine is older still. It took *homo erectus* no time at all to find herbs, mushrooms, seed pods, grasses, and leaves able to help him escape the everyday humdrum of mastodons and cave bears and intrusive cave-in-laws.

Other cultures altered consciousness not with pharmaceutical assistance but with rigorous disciplines of mind and body. Smoke lodges. Sweat lodges. Meditation. Chanting, rhythm, and music. Vibration. Activities pushing the human body to its physical limits and beyond. Ritual tattooing and mutilation. Crop offerings. Material offerings. Animal sacrifice. In some ancient cultures, human sacrifice.

Death, existential anxiety, the need for symbols and transcendence — somewhere along the way, these things merged to invite the emergence of spirituality and religion. Only human beings do this.

I pushed myself years ago to attempt a non-sectarian definition of spirituality. My goal was a definition broad enough to be universal

(I couldn't, for example, say "spirituality means being a Christian"), and concrete enough to be meaningful. (I refused insipid ideas such as "spirituality is whatever it means to *you*.")

So, for better or worse . . .

Spirituality is the intentional disciplines we undertake to realize, respond, and bear witness to essential relatedness.

What I learned in my effort was that I could not coin a meaningful definition without presupposing an article of faith. In the case of the above definition, I'm presupposing that people and things and events in this life are essentially related. I can't prove that. It's a part of my spiritual worldview leaking into my definition. A bad high school debate team would spot that in a minute.

(Can't apologize, however, because I *do* think things are essentially related.)

For me, healthy spirituality intercepts and overlaps my vision for competent mental health care: authenticity and human wholeness. I enjoy remembering that the Greek root hiding in the Christian idea of salvation is *sadzo*. From this root we derive words such as saved, salvation, holy, whole, authentic, health, and healing.

Healthy religion isn't about dodging the wrath of the gods, or about currying their favor. Healthy religion is about being properly related —to self, to neighbor, to community, to environment, to cosmos, and to the mystery (known to some folks as God).

Right relationships yield human wholeness.

Pastoral counselor considers spiritual dimension

A reader writes to ask me: **"What's pastoral counseling?"**

Measured by its recognition among traditional psychotherapy, pastoral counseling is a relative newcomer to the field of behavioral health. Though, seen another way, it's the oldest "counseling" of all.

Imagine a thousand years ago heading out of your tepee to sit down with the medicine man, or seeking the counsel of the village shaman or going to shrift in a twelfth century cathedral. Along with their institutional religious value, all these encounters could be thought of as a kind of behavioral health intervention.

In modern terms, most pastoral counselors have a similar core of clinical training as other master's-level therapists. But a pastoral counselor welcomes and includes the client/patient's understanding and interest in spirituality and sometimes in a particular religious practice. This, too, becomes part of the therapy. Pastoral counseling presupposes a relationship between healthy spirituality and mental health.

A skilled pastoral counselor helps people identify and clarify their understanding of their own spirituality. Pastoral counseling helps people make the best use of religious symbols. Pastoral counseling helps identify when religious practice is being misused for some destructive motive — when religion gets in the way of wholeness. Pastoral counseling provides a context in which people can distinguish between noble religious values and perhaps poisonous family or cultural teachings disguised as noble religious values.

Do you have to belong to a particular religion to make use of pastoral counseling? No, but don't be surprised if your pastoral counselor does belong to a particular religion. That does not mean your pastoral counselor will attempt to convert you to this faith or that faith. This is the huge — but often missed — difference between pastoral counseling and sectarian religious counseling.

A sectarian religious counselor brings to the table the clear assumption that this religion's "answer" is the right answer. For example, I have a friend who makes his living as a Christian counselor. He describes his job as "helping people find where they are in disagreement with God." My friend "counsels" people to agree with God, or at least agree with God as he understands God within the confines of his own Christian understanding. A sectarian religious counselor includes unabashed religious education, doctrinal persuasion, or even the hope to convert to a particular faith.

I don't want to imply that you can never talk to a traditional therapist about spirituality. The days of traditional therapy being inherently antagonistic to religion are mostly over. Secular therapy has matured enough to recognize both the value and the importance of religion and religious symbols. But a pastoral counselor has particular training in the language and symbols of faith and religious worldviews.

The Swiss psychiatrist Carl Jung agreed with Sigmund Freud that the sexual instinct and the death instinct are powerful forces in the world. But Jung made a significant contribution to the human discussion when he suggested that every human being also had a "religious instinct," the intuitive awareness that we need something more than merely ourselves to be whole.

I've always found it ironic that Freud, the great atheist, would choose the word "psychology" to describe his academic inquiry. Psychology means "the study of the soul."

What do we mean by forgiveness?

My friend scolds me for "not forgiving." But what exactly does he mean by forgiveness?

If by forgiveness he means I should let go of my anger, then okay. I get it. I agree with him. It's unhealthy to harbor bitterness, wrath, and enmity. So I forgive. In time, I'm not angry anymore. But what I notice is that forgiveness thus defined does not require an audience with those who treat me badly, or even that they be notified of my newfound peace. The entire transaction takes place within myself. It's about healing me.

Or if by forgiveness he means I surrender my claim upon restitution, that I never require any "pound of flesh" in payment for misdeeds, then okay. I get it. I agree with my friend. Moral inequities are part and parcel of a broken world, and we waste our lives if we insist on balancing every scale of justice. Besides, some deeds cannot be rectified. So I forgive. I let it go. But again I notice that forgiveness thus defined does not require me to engage my estranged and conflicted relationships. I can do this sort of forgiving by myself.

Perhaps by forgiveness my friend means I should relinquish my claim upon revenge. Okay again. I get it. I agree with him. I'm lousy at vengeance, and the desire for vengeance is soul-poison. So I forgive. I pledge that neither my action nor inaction will seek to harm those who do me wrong. And still this forgiveness is a spiritual exercise requiring no encounter whatsoever with a guilty human being.

But maybe my friend means all this and still more. He is asking me not only to surrender anger, restitution, and revenge, but also to make myself available and vulnerable again to the relationship in which I have been treated reprehensibly. A Christian man, he says this is what Jesus taught and modeled — a never-ending willingness to be vulnerable to sinners. And to that I say two things to my friend: 1) You're right about Jesus, and 2) I'm not Jesus.

So, in some cases, I withhold availability and vulnerability, and protect those same treasures with what I call a "holy resentment." This resentment is not indicative of spiritual ill-health or moral failure, but expresses instead a healthy self-respect. "Holy resentment" puts concerns about forgiveness on the back burner in favor of more pressing matters. I withhold availability and vulnerability — thus defined, I withhold forgiveness — until truth, contrition, and accountability make the question of forgiveness plausible and its possibility meaningful.

I once heard the story of a Protestant pastor whose counsel was sought by a woman with a black eye. The author of the black eye was the woman's husband. The pastor admonished the woman to be a "good Christian" and go home and forgive. She did. A month later her husband killed her.

How's this for provocative: Sometimes what we teach and admonish about forgiveness aids and abets evil. We need to know what we mean by forgiveness.

Carl Jung, monsters, and the rituals of Halloween

This afternoon I'll be up to my elbows in pumpkin guts with my three sons. We'll carve jack-o'-lanterns, and await Halloween. My four-year-old will don a Spider-Man outfit and comb the neighborhood extorting candy from folks (a treat) under the implied threat of vandalism (a trick). The only real trick Joseph knows, by the way, is grinning up at you and saying, "I want to tell you a secret." When you bend your head down to hear the secret, he will stick his tongue in your ear and run away laughing. Candy or wet willy: You've been warned.

Odd little custom, Halloween.

In our Western, Christian culture, of course, Halloween is short-hand for All Hallows' Eve. Meaning, the day before All Saints' Day. As the legend goes, demons and monsters and other beasties were especially active on October 31st because the power and piety of the Saints left them little room to maneuver on November 1st.

Some Christian groups are made especially anxious by Halloween, and see it as a tempting or consorting with evil. Their children will be kept home or consigned to church parties. Other folks are afraid their children will collect poisoned candy, or candy sabotaged with needles. Still other folks are offended in principle that they should have to shell out money for miniature boxes of Milk Duds and spend the evening answering the front door for an endless stream of ghosts, demons, monsters, and superheroes.

Whatever the case, every year more and more of my neighbors let their dark front porch announce to the world that they, too, have opted out of Halloween.

When I was a boy, my hobby was Aurora horror models. Boris Karloff as Frankenstein, Lon Chaney Jr. as the Wolf Man, Bela Lugosi as Dracula, The Mummy, Creature from the Black Lagoon, the Phantom of the Opera, Godzilla — all my favorite Saturday morning monster movies reduced to plastic, Testor paints, and model glue. For years these creatures of darkness and terror watched me sleep from their neatly choreographed perch on my bedroom bookshelf.

Did they scare me? Well, on one level, yes. I am attracted to classic monster myths the way other people are attracted to roller coasters. I enjoy the adrenaline rush of fear. But was I afraid of those monsters really? Nope. Quite the contrary. Looking back, I think they kept me from being scared.

Somehow, these monsters contained my fear. They expressed horror on my behalf. They helped me manage and articulate the parts of my universe that terrified me. And surely the most terrifying parts of my universe were not the threats around me, real or imagined; rather, the threats within me. I envied the monsters' uncensored rage. Bedlam. Wreaking havoc. The surrender to single-minded fury.

Okay, I need therapy.

All cultures have demon and monster myths. All cultures have customs and festivals in which people adorn themselves in costumes and make-up depicting demons and monsters. What's going on here? Is this reckless? Do we tempt the forces of darkness with these customs and rituals? Do we risk losing our souls to the evil and wickedness that demons and monsters perpetrate upon the world?

Carl Jung would have said it's just the opposite. He concluded that human beings share these customs universally because human beings share a universal need. To whit: A healthy human being must have access to every part of the self, even and especially our fantasies and desires about wickedness and evil. Demon and monster festivals are, at their core, an attempt to face the demons and the monsters within ourselves. To make them conscious. To stare them down. To take back our power over them.

Admitting evil makes evil less likely.

Or, said another way, I am much more comfortable in the company of a man wearing the mask of a demon than I am in the company of a demon wearing the mask of a man.

Why is religion arguing about sex and Jesus?

So I go to the local bookstore. On one side of the display is Dan Brown's book *The Da Vinci Code*. On the other side are all the spin-off titles responding to the popularity of Brown's book. *The Truth Behind the Da Vinci Code, Cracking Da Vinci's Code, Exploring the Da Vinci Code, Breaking the Da Vinci Code, The Da Vinci Hoax, Decoding Da Vinci* — it goes on and on.

Virtually all these titles (not to mention countless websites) have one thing in common: They understand themselves to be defending truth in the face of self-confessed fiction. They are defending Jesus. They are defending Christianity.

They are taking Dan Brown seriously.

Dan Brown's book says Jesus was married. Which I assume means he wasn't celibate. Which I assume means Jesus was a sexual being who had sex. According to *The Da Vinci Code*, this part of Jesus' history was hidden by the Church. According to *The Da Vinci Code*, if people ever knew that Jesus was a married, sexually active person, the power of the Church would be undermined and Christianity itself would collapse.

And if the tidal wave of refutations is any indication, many Christians agree wholeheartedly with Dan Brown's imaginative fancy. They don't agree Jesus was married and sexually active, mind you; they agree Christianity could be brought to its knees by proof that he was married and sexually active. Why else would we be drowning in this vociferous, indignant backlash?

If Jesus married and had sex, he certainly would not be a holy man. Certainly not the Christ of Christianity. Certainly not the definitive revelation of God. God — the author of sex — turns out to be deeply embarrassed by sex. God insists that truly holy people live without it.

One website rebutting Brown's novel tells me "the Jesus of the Bible is holy, upright, and sinless." Does that mean every non-celibate is unholy, bent, and sinful? Why and how did we tie holiness to sexlessness?

I'm astonished by religious people who feel the need to offer apology to fiction, as I would be if the local mortuary mobilized community education efforts in response to the film release of *Night of the Living Dead*. (Don't be fooled! We guarantee your loved one will stay right where we buried them!) And what if these religious folks are right? Are Americans so absent reality contact and true spirituality that they are actually turning to popular novels for serious religious education?

But what disturbs me most is the widely accepted idea that sexuality is antithetical to spirituality and true holiness; that there is, in the end, no way to be holy and randy at the same time.

If I had to list the top three reprehensible tragedies of religion in the last two thousand years, somewhere in the top two would be the way religion has made human beings profoundly miserable and crippled about sex. This tragedy happens because of the way religion tends — incredibly and unnecessarily — to presuppose an inherent antagonism between sexuality and spirituality.

I'm not being funny: It's no accident that, during crucial moments of human intimacy, the words most commonly uttered are "Oh God." Sexuality and spirituality are not necessary antagonists. It's a lie.

Was Jesus married? Personally, I rather doubt it. Was Jesus sexually active? That's his business. None of that is my point. Please resist the temptation to write me and make sure I think the right things about Jesus.

Here's my point: The world would be a happier, safer, kinder, more creative, and less violent place if more of us were having better sex more often.

There. I said it.

Some religion just adds to the misery of others

I'm trying to wrap my mind around the religious folks telling me that hurricanes are God's Judgment. Pat Robertson (*700 Club*) says it's about abortion. Charles Colson (*BreakPoint*) says it's to warn us about readiness for terrorist attacks. Hal Lindsay says it's a more general move harkening the last days of the late, great planet Earth. At escapeallthesethings.com, I'm told it's because of U.S. political pressure on Israel to surrender the Gaza Strip to Palestine. Or try repentamerica.com, where hurricanes are explained as God's particular need to punish New Orleans for its unique decadence.

And here I thought Disneyland was uniquely decadent.

Myriad interpretations, but all these folks agree on one thing: God's Judgment.

So I wrap my mind around all that, and come to this conclusion: God is a terrible shot. Worst I've ever seen. Mind-bogglingly bad.

His last couple of tosses started off with promise. It's no mean feat to throw a hurricane from the Western coast of Africa up and over Cuba yet underneath Florida against the Gulf Stream current and into the Gulf of Mexico. It's really hard to do, and God has done it twice in a row. Yeah, for a while there it looked like God was going to redeem Himself from last season, when his attempts to punish the city of New Orleans kept sailing high and bouncing off the hotels and condos of Florida retirees.

No; things look good as God slides Katrina into the gulf and on toward the sinners of New Orleans. But the pitch gets away from him and wipes a few Mississippi towns off the map ("Sorry . . ."), and then a bit of Alabama ("Pardon me . . . sorry"), and then drowns some elderly people in a rest home ("Terribly sorry . . ."). God is like the John Cleese portrayal of Sir Lancelot in the film *Monty Python and the Holy Grail*. Lancelot kills thirty or forty innocent wedding guests on the way to the castle tower, and when confronted with the carnage says politely, "Sorry, it's just that when I'm in this particular idiom, I tend to get carried away."

Hurricane Rita was a classic case of God throwing a pitch before He really knew what He wanted to do with it. Again, it starts well. Into the Gulf. Category Five. Looking . . . looking . . . waiting. But too late God sees that He's not exactly sure where all the New Orleans sinners have fled. Galveston? Corpus Christi? The Yucatan Peninsula? Did they double back to the Big Easy? And as God hesitates, the hurricane crashes into Lake Charles, Louisiana, a city not known for either a preponderance of transvestites or strong opinions about Israel.

Remember when God tried to punish gay men in San Francisco with HIV? By the time that was over, He'd infected much of Africa, most of Haiti, and six dentists on the Eastern seaboard. He killed my friend Chris, who, as near as I can tell, was the second-to-last hemophiliac in line to receive untested blood transfusions in the mid-'80s ("So sorry . . ."). Hear me now — He was aiming at San Francisco. And He hit *Africa*. Another continent entirely.

I'm calling for God's retirement. I think He should get out of the Judgment business.

Of course, there is one other possible conclusion: Not all religious ideology is useful. Or healthy. Or even safe. Some religious ideas are worse than wrong. They are wicked and dangerous. Some religions add misery to people already miserable, and add self-righteous aggrandizement to folks already possessed by a critical mass of hubris.

The car in front of me has a bumper sticker that says, "In case of

Rapture, this car will be unmanned." Hope it doesn't careen into my son's preschool.

Bad religion can happen in any religion

When I'm channel surfing, my favorite wave to catch is the Comedy Channel. Some of the comics are obnoxious. Some are just unfunny. But occasionally, some are brilliant.

A while back I caught a Native American comic. This guy made me laugh until I was wiping tears. And he really only had one target for his clever satire: Christianity.

Specifically, he went on and on, straining and exaggerating the picture of Jesus and the message of the Christian Gospel and its historical interaction with aboriginal Americans. Lampoon, to be sure, but this guy mixed in just enough of the historical and political truth to make it funny. Because, in the end, only the truth is funny.

He wrapped it up by thanking the Los Angeles audience, and saying that, a few weeks earlier, this same stuff didn't go over so well in Texas. He said he was confronted after the show by two huge cowboys who blocked his exit, stuck out their jaws and said, "We're Christians, and we don' like the way you were talkin' 'bout Jeezshus."

"Yeah?" the comic deadpanned. "So forgive me."

Oh, the irony.

I've been drawn to Internet news services these past few weeks, absorbing everything I can get my hands on about a series of editorial cartoons published in a Danish newspaper, and then reprinted in assorted newspapers around the world. The cartoons depicted the prophet Muhammad. In one frame, Muhammad is wearing a bomb as a hat. The Islamic world is outraged.

But what exactly did these cartoons mercilessly lampoon? Islam? The actual man Muhammad? Muhammad's actual message? Muslims?

I don't think so. Just like I don't think the Native American comic was talking about Jesus. No, the comic used the name and narratives of Jesus as props to make a brutal observation, the same observation these cartoons appear to make: Few things are more potentially lethal than people who cannot psychologically distinguish between God and their own infantile ego needs. More simply, bad religion exacerbates the already breathtaking human propensity for hatred and violence.

And bad religion can happen in any religion. *Any* religion. No prophet or teacher is safe from conscription in service to fear, narcissism, and megalomania. Not Muhammad. Not Jesus. No one. Hiding our love for violence behind our love for God is not an Islamic disease. It's a human disease.

Here's an excerpt from a CNN news story:

"Up to 300 hard-line Islamic activists in Indonesia, the world's most populous Muslim country, went on a rampage in the lobby of a building housing the Danish embassy in Jakarta. Shouting "Allahu Akbar" (God is greatest), they smashed lamps with bamboo sticks, threw chairs, lobbed rotten eggs and tomatoes and tore up a Danish flag."

Isn't it interesting when people vehemently protest an unflattering observation, and, in an effort to render that protest, begin behaving in precisely the way that drew the critical observation in the first place?

It embarrasses me to watch the Ku Klux Klan use the name of Jesus to advance its cause. I cringe to know that a church in Kansas once sponsored a website called www.godhatesfags.com. I want to hide under a blanket when I hear U.S. leaders allude to religious values to explain their inspiration for "freeing the Iraqi people" and use that same explanation for why we just shouldn't get involved in, say, Rwandan genocide.

Is it too much to hope that faithful Muslims are embarrassed by folks using the name of Muhammad to wrap themselves in explosives and go for bus rides?

Mocking beloved religious figures is bad form and prejudicial, and deserves public censure. But make no mistake, the perversion of religion in service to violence *deserves* to be satirized.

I'm playing four-on-four basketball at the park. My opponent misses a point-blank, uncontested layup. In the next few seconds, my opponent mentions the name of Jesus at least five times. In my opponent's diatribe, Jesus is adverb, adjective, verb, proper noun, and, well, very busy. It's foul. Unpleasant. Makes me wince. Offends my Christian sensibilities. Makes me glad my son didn't come to the park with me.

But it never once occurs to me to cut his head off so that God can be glorified.

Remembering mortality could lead to more fulfilled life

Myrrh is mine; its bitter perfume
Breathes a life of gathering gloom
Sorrowing, sighing, bleeding, dying
Sealed in the stone-cold tomb

— JOHN HENRY HOPKINS JR.

You might not know Mr. Hopkins by name, but he authored the song-version of the story of The Magi in the Christian Gospel of Matthew. He's famous for the poetic complication of the simple sentence, "We are three Kings from the Orient." He preferred "We three Kings of Orient are." And his song always makes me want to say . . .

And a Merry Christmas to you, too, Mr. Hopkins. Nice song. Remind me not to invite you to any of my holiday parties. Whatever happened to "Tis the season to be jolly"? I know songwriters tend to be a depressed lot, but don't you know this is the time of year for socially mandated happiness?

Or so I would have thought until a few years ago.

Don was my boyhood neighbor. Later, he was my basketball buddy. A quite minor inconvenience was that he was a better athlete than I was. Three days after Christmas 2002, Don was browsing the aisles at Home Depot. Witnesses say he twice exclaimed "Oh my God," then collapsed to the floor, where he died. Don was forty-one. Straight arrow. Didn't drink. Didn't smoke. His wife and three sons miss him terribly.

I hate that Don is dead, and a quite major inconvenience is that Don died seven years younger than I am now. And I wasn't the only one at the funeral pondering mortality. The pews were filled with a fair handful of my dumbstruck peers. One high school classmate was being neither funny nor disrespectful when he muttered, "Geez, Don. Home Depot? If that's the way I go out, I hope I'm shopping at Victoria's Secret!" Wry. But my friend was deadly serious. Maybe even he didn't know how serious.

The Three Wise Men bring gold, frankincense, and myrrh to celebrate Jesus' birth. Now, gold is obvious. Great gift. The incense is a little "out there" maybe, but it makes a good stocking stuffer for New Age baby boomer parents. But what's the deal with the myrrh? A pungent, gum-resin balm used to bury the dead? That would be the same myrrh used to mask the stench of decay? To celebrate the birth of a child? This is either the most tasteless, thoughtless Christmas present of all time, or . . .

. . . the perfect gift. Only mortals are born. Every new life is celebrated in the context of death. Every significant religion has in common an attempt to wrench meaning from the astonishing fact that some day we lie down and do not get back up. Healthy cultures (not ours) turn youth into adults precisely with rites of passage communicating unabashedly, "You're gonna die, bud." Oh, the Wise Men get it. We live better when we are humbly and dynamically related to our mortality.

The last time I went to Home Depot, I came back with garden mulch and a big, gray, plastic garbage can. The last time Don went to Home Depot, he didn't come back at all. There's no reason that my three sons have a living father and Don's do not. The Buddhists say that every day spent not contemplating one's own death is a wasted day. The Christian version of that same sentiment quotes God as saying "You fool! This very night you will have to give up your life; then who will get all these things you have kept for yourself?"

New Year's resolutions for 2006:

• Waste fewer days.

• Give away more.

• Worry less about yourself.

Sweat lodge ordeal triggers brief spiritual experience

It's still dark when I arrive in the wee hours of morning at the sweat lodge. I had begun to worry that I was lost, but you can't miss the giant flames of the bonfire shooting into the beckoning arms of a dawning winter solstice.

It's cold. I'm standing on red clay and old snowfall somewhere on the Kaibab Indian Reservation north of the Grand Canyon. Absurdly quiet. The sound of my own crunching footsteps is dwarfed, as if coming from an old AM radio. The sky seems bigger out here. Or I seem smaller.

Funny how things happen. A friend called and insisted I meet Ben, a tribal elder and spiritual leader. Ben interviewed me at my kitchen table. I passed muster. He invited me to the sweat lodge. And here I am, out in the middle of nowhere. White Guy from Town.

Cars and trucks trickle in. Soon I'm surrounded by eighteen or twenty Paiutes and one other nervous white guy. I receive instruction from the Firekeeper about the lodge. The altar. Here's how we properly enter the lodge. Here's how we exit.

My first thought as I enter the darkness of the lodge is how this many people are going to fit in here. Like sardines, that's how. Smells like human being in here. I deny the first stirring of claustrophobia.

A maybe twelve-year-old Paiute girl sits next to her mother. (Ben is controversial, because he allows men and women to "sweat" together. But not if the women are menstruating, because then they are too powerful.) In the firelight, the girl's countenance is unmistakable. Sullen. Resentful. Wow, cool piece of cross-cultural universalism. I recognize that look. It's identical to the look my children give me when I announce that it's time to get ready for church.

There's an earthen depression in the center of the lodge. Using a pitchfork, the Firekeeper removes igneous rocks from the bonfire and brings them into the lodge. He drops them one by one into the pit. The rocks pulse white and red. Heat builds and moves the air around me. It's primordial. At once ancient and new. Like peeking into the earth's core. Like having a front-row seat on the day of Creation.

Ben sprinkles herbs on the rocks. They jump and crackle in a miniature Whoville Fourth of July fireworks display. Then he dips a tie of sage into a pot of water and shakes it into the rocks.

The flap goes down. The dark swallows us. It begins.

The steam bounces off the rocks. The heat rises immediately and exponentially, attacking me. The earlier claustrophobia is now a budding panic. Breathing is difficult. In some detached place in my brain, I wonder how often Goofy White Guys from Town die in sweat lodge ceremonies. I wonder if in a few moments I'll launch myself screaming and clawing right through the branches and fabric of this makeshift hut.

That's when some huge native hand engulfs the back of my head and pushes my face down between my knees. Was he psychic? Or have they learned over the months and years that White Guys from Town won't figure out for themselves the air is cooler and more breathable down toward the ground? Either way I am grateful, and my panic abates.

Then the song erupts. Whatever your favorite Hollywood stereotype of native voices chanting loudly in native tongue, well, multiply by one thousand and wrap it around my head in quadraphonic stereo in a very small, enclosed space in the pitch dark. It takes me apart. Shatters me. A beautiful, terrible din.

When the flap lifts, I crawl out of the lodge on my hands and knees, my sweat mixing with the red dirt. I suck in the cold air and squint at the sun just clearing the horizon. I look like a photo from *National Geographic*. Or like a freshman pledge after a hazing. Or roadkill.

And that was the first of four rounds.

Catholic Christians speak of seven sacraments, but serious spirituality should require an eighth: The Ordeal. A spiritual discipline requiring effort, rigor, surrender to discomfort. Making extreme demands of the body so the mind might stop wandering off in self-indulgent ego-dreams.

I drive back to Las Vegas thoughtful, exhausted, quiet. See, in Round Three, I had a religious experience. For a moment — a very brief moment — I saw, I felt, I knew . . . how the willingness to accept suffering in one's own body can extend healing and peace into the world.

The experience vanished as quickly as it came. Next thing you know, you're back in Las Vegas at an all-you-can-eat buffet.

Healthy religion strives for human wholeness

A reader writes to ask me: **"Are you for or against religion? I see that you are a pastoral counselor, yet your columns often seem critical of religion."**

For. Absolutely passionate about it. Which is why I am so often critical of it. Because it matters so much to me.

Distorted religion or religion in the hands of distorted personalities is perhaps the most dangerous and violent force in the universe. On its smaller scales, it has the capacity to ruin individual lives by surrounding those lives with quiet misery. On larger scales it provides the impetus for such marquee human phenomena as child abuse, economic injustice, and genocide.

You'd better believe I'm critical.

I've said before that Freud, the presumed great atheist, might have made the original "Freudian slip" when he called his new academic investigation "psychology" — the study of the soul. Didn't know atheists believed in souls, Siggy.

But competent psychology and competent religion have at least one goal in common: the hope of human wholeness. In the Christian Gospels, for example, you'll frequently find the word "salvation." It derives from a Greek root *sadzo*, the same root giving rise to words such as holy, healthy, whole, authentic. Whatever else Christians mean by "being saved," it seems to me that a salvific event is an event that opens the door to authentic human wholeness.

But since Freud, religion and psychology have been nemesis to the other's hubris. If you've written me to say that you think you notice me enjoying the role of nemesis, then you've got me dead to rights. It's a fair cop. I'm busted. I admit to being very reactive to emotional dishonesty, to the disguising of self-serving or even malicious motives as piety or value. And when I think an individual or an institution is conscripting the rights and liberties of others just so they can continue the luxury of dodging self-examination, well, I'm usually going to want to talk about it. Out loud.

But don't you see that I do that precisely because of my love for true religion, its beauty and values?

Carl Jung agreed with Freud that the instincts for sex and violence are real. But he diverged from Freud when he said that the fundamental instinct inside the human being was the "religious instinct." By that he meant the innate yearning to reach beyond the mere self toward a greater wholeness. I agree with Jung. Everyone has this yearning.

Even destructive behavior often reveals some desire for human transcendence. Take alcoholism, for example. It's no accident they call that stuff "spirits." Drinking is a kind of distorted spirituality. M. Scott Peck, famous for *The Road Less Traveled*, came to postulate that addicts were deeply spiritual people whose spirituality had been distorted into compulsive behavior.

Religion is a Latin word: *religare*. It means "to bind together." Healthy religion provides the narratives, symbols, and ceremonies binding together meaning, values, and relationships. Healthy religion provides a dynamic context in which people can be born, develop, become, and die in the hope of a growing wholeness and authenticity.

What follows is a short list of my prejudices about what distinguishes healthy and unhealthy religion:

- Healthy religion recognizes the developmental stages of a maturing spirituality, and encourages the movement through those stages. Unhealthy religion impedes that development, and shames or vilifies those who attempt to move from one stage to the next.

- Healthy religion is not threatened by passion, be that creative passion, artistic passion, sexual passion, or celebration. Unhealthy religion is afraid of such things, and moves subtly or aggressively to constrain, punish, or ostracize passionate people.

- Healthy religion is not anti-intellectual. Unhealthy religion is afraid of certain questions.

- Healthy religion values truth more than it values being right.

- Healthy religion respects and values both male and female. Unhealthy religion tends to be marked by the oppressive masculine or the critical, shaming feminine. (Dana Carvey's *Saturday Night Live* character "The Church Lady" wouldn't be funny if it wasn't true.)

- The goal of healthy religion is wholeness, and the freedom wholeness invites. The goal of unhealthy religion (regardless of what they say) is control and conformity. Its favorite strategy to this end is constantly cultivating in you ambivalence, doubts, or even hatred for the self.

Unhealthy religion is a bully. And if I sound a little grouchy sometimes about religion, it's because I hate bullies.

The yin and yang of unsolicited messages

Home from work, and the ritual begins:

From under my windshield wiper I remove a flier inviting me to lose weight. I collect from the front doorknob an offer from a real estate agency to sell my house. Folded into my patio gate is a menu from a Thai restaurant. In the bushes is a menu for pizza and wings. (Maybe they think digging trash out of my bushes will make me hungry.)

On to the mailbox. With a practiced hand I remove the wad of paper therein and head for the waste basket. The flier and the menus are trashed, quickly followed by offers to clean my carpet, kill my bugs, and give me long, beautiful fingernails.

My phone rings maybe three to seven times each evening because some concerned caller (or concerned computer) wants to know how I've managed to survive without a Kirby Vacuum, solar heater, or

Amway distributorship. Would I like to earn twenty-seven buh-jillion dollars per month in only ten minutes per day sitting at my kitchen table in my underwear? Some people will be in my neighborhood next week testing the local tap water. You won't believe this, but those same people are coincidentally prepared to sell me water treatment devices on the off chance my tap water turns out to be mostly a cocktail of sludge, jet fuel, and catfish droppings.

Ding-dong. The youth at my door wants me to buy overpriced candy, and murmurs something about how my purchase keeps him "off the streets and out of trouble." (If I buy a chocolate bar, you won't come back with spray paint and tag my garage door?) The next youth has real urgency in her voice, and tells me she is just a few magazine subscriptions away from going to Disneyland. (Is there no end to the collapse of values in America? How am I going to get through the evening thinking this young lady might not get to Disneyland?) Next are the folks who drop by to announce that my religion is ALL screwed up and, lucky for me, they can fix all that with THEIR religion, which, it turns out, is the correct and not-screwed-up religion. Okay then.

Finally, around nine p.m. there is peace. The world of unsolicited advertising is at rest until another day. (Mostly at rest, anyway. According to my e-mail spam, I'm not consuming anywhere near my rightful share of Xanex.)

Don't you HATE unsolicited advertising? Don't you deeply resent the idea that someone or something else knows better than you what you need and want? Shouldn't the universe wait for us to ask for what we need?

Well, maybe when it comes to clean carpets and Thai food, but before you get carried away, try this little exercise in humility: Count up the top twenty blessings and treasures of your life, and notice how many of them you never consciously sought or even knew you desired. Before their arrival, you did not miss them, or even consider that you needed them. They just showed up, unsolicited. And, having shown up, you don't know how you could understand your life without them.

I didn't ask my father to teach me responsible use of money, a work ethic, and the value of citizenship; he offered the wisdom unsolicited. I didn't know I needed to learn that every human being has an inherent dignity deserving of my respect; my mother shared this truth unsolicited. My wife is not the woman of my dreams. She is the woman about whom I could not dream . . . did not know how to dream. She came to my life unsolicited — while I was looking for some other woman.

How sad and empty our lives would be if the universe waited for us to recognize our deepest needs and ask for them. We're just not that smart.

Hope is a beautiful and dangerous thing

Hope feeds us. Nurtures us. When we live hopefully, we live expectantly. We don't know what is going to happen, but that doesn't stop us from expecting things to happen.

Hopeful people are always looking, ready, waiting, expecting. Each morning is like an Easter egg hunt. Things might look normal and mundane, but someone has tucked and hidden beautiful things under and around obvious and everyday places. Sometimes the beautiful thing is tucked under tragedy and suffering.

Hope is sometimes a gift. Sometimes it just happens. It opens inside us and around us like a rose's bloom in time-lapse photography. We feel it, and are thankful for it. Other times hope is a discipline, which is to say a choice. I don't mean the childish folly of "everything will be okay," because everything is not okay and some things will never be okay. No; hope as discipline is the decision to move forward expectantly even and after our worst fears are realized. The risk of hope is the willingness to look even into devastation for the possibility of meaning and new life — a life worth living.

Despair is a kind of grief. Specifically, despair is the name of that sorrow that results from the loss of hope. Hopelessness is a profound loss indeed, perhaps a human being's most terrifying and painful loss. Yet, ironically, most hopeless people don't feel hopeless; they behave hopelessly. Their despair isn't apparent to them as despair;

their behavior despairs. They live their lives just the other side of "Que sera, sera." It's more like, so life stinks and then you die and I no longer give a tinker's damn. Let's party.

In the Stephen King short story "Rita Hayworth and the Shawshank Redemption," protagonists Andy and Red are prison inmates and fast friends. Yet the harshest words they ever exchange are over a disagreement about hope. "Hope is a dangerous thing in here," Red says venomously.

"You're wrong about hope," Andy insists. "Hope is a good thing, one of life's best things." Red storms away from the table.

But Red is not despairing. His hostility toward hope reveals its beckoning presence. And Red is correct. Hope *is* dangerous. While hope opens us to life's richest experiences, it also makes us most vulnerable to being made a fool. The human ego reacts badly to shattered hope.

So Red is clinging desperately to the ego's remedy for both despair and hope — cynicism. And as bad as cynicism feels, and as dull and boring as it makes us, we experience it as a victory over foolishness. We're back in charge. In charge of what, exactly, I'm not sure. Our own defiant emptiness?

The doctor tells the man he has cancer. How serious, we don't yet know. Time for tests. Time to sit around and pretend things are normal while somebody in a lab decides whether or not he's dying.

"We'll have these test results back in about a week," the nurse says.

"No problem," thinks the man. "I'll just be at home . . . waiting."

But he isn't just home waiting. He goes home to smoke all the more. Smoke like a fiend. He'll show those doctors who's boss. He'll be damned before he'll be foolish enough to hope for a cure. To hope for life. To hope for meaning even if there is no cure. To hope.

There is a new pseudo-spirituality out there that goes something like this: Don't burden people with your expectations of them. Don't get invested in any particular outcome. "I don't expect anything," says one such guru, "that way I'm never disappointed."

Well, it appears some of us will remain spiritually unenlightened.

Most married people, for example, hope and expect their spouses will endure, will not discard them, will not lie to them or betray them in adultery. Furthermore, to be married is to have a deep investment in those particular outcomes.

If I ever tell you that I have no expectations of you, it won't be a compliment. It will mean that I'm done. Through. Divested.

People in therapy often ask, "Is there any hope?"

The fact that you made this appointment is evidence of hope. The fact that you're still asking that question.

Resolutions have good intentions, sorry track record

So you did it. About five minutes until midnight yesterday, you smoked the last cigarette of your life. Yeah, you could have stopped on a random Monday afternoon in October, or on your mother-in-law's birthday, but there's nothing like the power of a New Year's resolution to change lives.

And you have lots of company. The resolution business is booming today. Tons of folks, for example, are heading for the gym. Maybe you, like me a few years ago, reached into your stocking and pulled out a membership as a loving gift from your spouse. "How sweet," I thought, until suddenly it hit me.

"Is this a Christmas present," I asked my wife, "or an editorial?" She pursed her lips and shrugged. I went to the gym. Couldn't believe what I saw in the mirror . . . or on the scale. Thank God the place was packed with doughy, sweaty, middle-aged people huffing and puffing. I didn't stick out — at least not until I almost passed out in the shower.

Big buff guy: "You okay?"

Me: "Fine. I always shower with my head between my knees."

Then there are those of you who have resolved to stop cursing. No more potty mouth. I have relatives who would be rendered mute by this exercise. Without bad language, they wouldn't have sufficient vocabulary to ask directions to the restroom. But good luck to you. Give 'em hell. Uh, sorry. Make that heck. I give you until January 9th, tops.

This morning there also will be a few unscheduled resolutions regarding alcoholic beverages. These life-changing oaths will come from folks clutching the linoleum floors of bathrooms, wondering why the drummer from last night's bar band followed them home. Temporal lobe Grey Goose vodka sledgehammer headache in stereo. You'd have to get better to die.

"Can I bring you anything to eat, maybe settle your stomach?" I once asked my desperately hungover college roommate, curled like a winning horseshoe around the commode. "A cube of butter? Cold Pop-Tart? Open a can of smoked oysters?"

And that was it for my roommate's New Year's resolution to stop cursing.

Change is a funny thing. I know it's possible. Just don't have a clue how it works. A few folks will actually and permanently stop smoking today. Maybe five or six of the new faces at my gym this afternoon will still be showing up in April. Almost all of you on the linoleum floor will be hungover a few more times before you decide you're no longer having any fun.

Why the anemic track record? Why do so many resolutions fail to reach orbit and fall haplessly back to Earth?

Resolutions for change are about intention and effort. But the consistent irony is change requires *more* than intention and effort. Some third mystery ingredient. What is the magic additive? Is it readiness? Enlightenment? Grace? The latest CDs and workbooks from some loud geek on an infomercial?

I swear I don't know. I only know that many of my best-intentioned efforts to remake myself have ultimately not been fruitful. Which doesn't mean I've never made significant changes in my life, only that, when I have made changes, it has often felt more like something that happened to me. Not something I did to myself.

My father quit smoking about ten years before he died. He had tried to quit scores of times before. But one day his five-year-old grandson confronted him and his lit cigarette on a back patio. "If you keep smoking, Grandpa, you're going to die," the old soul kindergartener observed. My dad paused. Snuffed out the cigarette on the balcony railing. Never picked up a cigarette again.

Who knows how change happens? All we can do is keep coming up with the intention and effort until it does.

Taking issue with *The Secret*: It is naked hubris, pure and simple

Readers keep asking me about *The Secret*. It's available in book and movie form. Here's a good general rule about hanging with me: Never ask me anything you don't want to know.

Check out *The Secret's* official website. "The Great Secret of the universe . . . has been passed throughout the ages, traveling through centuries, to reach you and humankind. This is The Secret to everything — the secret to unlimited joy, health, money, relationships, love, youth . . ."

What exactly is unlimited youth? Will I have to be nervous around girls forever? Will I always have the brains of a sheep, the historical perspective of a housefly, and the impulse control of a hamster? Tell me again why I want this?

The Secret is just the newest packaging for the most ancient and pervasive burden of being human: egocentricity and its inevitable companion, narcissism. We used to call it magic. In orthodox religious circles, its name is Gnosticism. It's officially modern name is logocentrism.

"Logo," from the Greek *logos*, meaning of the mind, a thought or idea. Put simply, logocentrism is the idea that all reality is first an idea or thought. Indeed, the thought actually creates or attracts the reality.

Rene Descarte said "I think, therefore I am." Logocentrists say, "I think, therefore it *is*." Magicians say "abracadabra." Christians seduced by logocentrism (who should know better) say "in the name of Jesus" for the same reason.

Is there power in positive thinking? Yes. Relative power, but powerful. Its primary power is that it makes us more aware of and willing to risk potentials and possibilities.

Yet, negative thinking does NOT prevent me (sometimes) from receiving unexpected and perfect gifts "from the universe." In fact, while *The Secret* prompts me to will, want, and visualize as a strategy for making cool things happen, I would say I have just as often made cool things happen by the simple act of giving up.

Or maybe cool things happen independently from whether I think positively or negatively. Maybe cool things don't care what I think. Maybe I'm just not that big a deal.

The Secret is naked hubris, pure and simple.

"Perception is reality," my friend says, eyeing me with a benevolent condescension that waits for me to stop resisting and join her in enlightenment. "Tell that to John F. Kennedy Jr.," I say.

See, according to the evidence, John Jr. thought, with every fiber of his being, that he was flying level to the horizon. But he wasn't. And his thinking otherwise didn't make it so. When he turned into his approach pattern, he pretty much pointed the nose of his plane straight into the Atlantic. Might as well have been in a trash compactor. He died, as did his passengers.

Are the producers of *The Secret* going to tell me that John Jr. was secretly "blocking" the possibility of flying level with the horizon? And what happens when half the passengers are visualizing flying safely and half visualize crashing?

When religion gets hold of *The Secret's* secret, then it's God who wants us to have everything. Salvation is equated with limitlessness. Everybody ought to be rich, free of pain, and just plain hip all the time. Which is the same as saying if you're poor, in pain, and unhip, then it's your fault. You're a screw-up. What is it about you that you won't simply *decide* to stop having cancer?

Do the poor participate in their own poverty? In many cases, yes. Is most of our misery related in some way to our choices? Uh-huh. But that's just it. One of the limits inherent in being human is that I can't *not* make choices that impoverish me and make me miserable.

The Secret says everybody ought to be rich. Healthy religion would say everybody ought to have the chance to be wholly and authentically human.

Is there virtually always more potential around you than you think there is? Yes. Are you responsible for or at minimum participating in virtually all your misery? Yes. Are you inherently lazy? Often. Are many of your "limitations" self-imposed? Definitely.

But are you God?

I feel an obligation to tell you a secret. It has been passed throughout the ages, traveling through the centuries to reach you and humankind. You have my permission to share this secret with anyone, anytime, anywhere.

No. You're not God.

Teaching human wholeness outside the institution

A reader writes to ask me: "You have mentioned in previous columns being a former member of the ordained clergy. Why former? Are you still involved in church work today?"

In the nine months since we added Tuesday's *Asking Human Matters* to my regular Sunday column, yours is the sixth time I've been asked this question. I didn't respond the first five times. Not sure why I'm responding now.

Am I still involved in church work? In the broader sense, the work I'm doing today is virtually identical to my previous life as a parish priest. I provide people a context of meaning, safety, and encouragement in which to confront themselves, learn, suffer, celebrate, grow. I teach. I communicate a vision of human wholeness and authenticity.

Same vocation. Different location. Different audience. And so much more room to breathe.

But if you're asking specifically if I'm any longer serving institutional religion in a professional capacity, the answer is "no." I've returned to civilian life, as it were.

Why?

Ever read Ken Kesey's 1962 novel *One Flew Over the Cuckoo's Nest*? Or seen the film adaptation starring Jack Nicholson? The setting is among the patients and workers in a mental institution.

In Kesey's story, you meet our hero, R.P. McMurphy, a con man who pretends to be a mental health case to avoid a prison work farm. He challenges authority. He teaches the mental patients to be sane.

You also meet Nurse Ratched, the ward superintendent. You don't like her. Kesey describes her as "enormous, capable of swelling up bigger and bigger to monstrous proportions." As you keep reading, you wonder if she's a very good psych nurse. Pages later, you wonder if she's helping the patients. Still later, you wonder if she's hurting the patients.

But it is worse still than all that. In the end, you discover that Nurse Ratched needs the patients to be sick. She conscripts the patients to maintain the polished persona necessary to avoid confronting her own injured and insecure self.

Billy is a thirty-one-year-old stuttering neurotic. McMurphy sneaks two prostitutes onto the ward late at night, one of whom spends the night with Billy. When Nurse Ratched arrives on the scene the next morning, she is outraged. Billy comes hopping out of his room, pulling on his pants, to the applause of the other patients.

"Aren't you ashamed of yourself?" asks Nurse Ratched, her voice dripping with the very shame she so desperately needs Billy to wear. And for the first time in his life, in the company of a powerful woman, Billy, utterly sane, sets his gaze and says, without stuttering, "No, ma'am."

I'm not advocating sex workers as part of the regular treatment plan for psych patients, but who cannot see this tawdry romp has been a healing intervention for Billy? He is in this moment wholly himself.

Off balance for but a few seconds, you can see the feral intelligence of a new idea bloom behind the nurse's eyes. "Well," she says smugly. "We'll see what your mother has to say about this."

Billy begins to stutter again. He begs Nurse Ratched not to tell his mother. They take him back to his room, screaming. Billy breaks a glass and cuts his own throat. He kills himself.

Only McMurphy sees the evil as evil. He jumps on Nurse Ratched. Attempts to choke her to death. For his trouble, he gets a lobotomy.

But I think McMurphy's real crisis happens earlier in the book. Nurse Ratched leads group therapy. McMurphy is dumbfounded, incredulous to learn that he is the only patient in this hospital who is remanded there. Every one else is free — totally free — to leave the hospital at any time. But they don't leave. They remain passive. In effect, they agree to both obedience and unwellness because they are, in the end, just as invested in Nurse Ratched's persona as she is.

No one cares. This is McMurphy's real horror. His unspeakable pain.

Thus endeth my little allegory.

I didn't leave because of Nurse Ratched. I left because it finally occurred to me that, collectively speaking, everyone was just fine with Nurse Ratched.

I left before they gave me a lobotomy.

Observing Matters

HUMANS ARE FOOLISH. If you don't believe me, consider that every day Americans order and eat something called an Egg McMuffin. They actually say "Egg McMuffin" out loud to an intercom speaker on a huge menu that includes a photo of an Egg McMuffin.

Foolish, I say. Imagine explaining the sport of boxing to someone from another planet: "Well, in boxing, there are these two people who hit each other with their fists. The object is to so severely injure your opponent's brain that he falls down and can't get back up."

Human beings style and groom their pubic hair.

Ever really think about the origin of cheese? First, it had to occur to somebody to be curious about what would happen if you walked over and pulled on the teats of some innocent ungulate bystander. See, right there I would say you don't have enough to occupy your mind. But that's what happened, and the Milking Ungulates Industry was born. Sheep, goats, cows, horses, llamas, yaks, (the milking of hippos was a total bust), impalas, camels — never dawned on any-one, I guess, that we were the only mammals on the planet who still wanted to drink this stuff after infancy.

But cheese? Somebody looked at a bowl of fresh milk, and said, "Not so fast. What if we don't drink it? What if we just let it sit here for four or five days?" Or maybe they set the bowl on the mantle and got distracted. Forgot about it. Came back and found it curdled.

Either way, I don't get it. You ever smelled curdled milk? Good *God.* Wouldn't a reasonable person have grimaced, retched, and thrown the foul stuff away? But no! They grimaced, retched . . . and then decided it might be good to eat.

Yep. Foolish. Men generally eschew intimate touch with other men, except in the case of congratulating a teammate for a job well done in a sporting contest, in which case they proceed to spank, swat, cup, squeeze, caress, cradle, and otherwise fondle their teammate's bum. I mean, why not knead the muscles around the lumbar vertebrae, or pinch the cheek with the thumb and forefinger? Nope, athletic celebrations have evolved to focus on a guy's ass.

Consider all the flora on planet Earth that have leaves that could be trimmed from the plant, dried, crumpled up, and then set on fire. Who first wondered what would happen if we deliberately inhaled the smoke from the fire into our lungs? And, after spewing and coughing and getting their eyes to stop watering, what made them think it would be a good idea to do it again?

Deliberately inhaling smoke must be some primordial biological drive. It explains why, as a kid, my older sister and I once got into my mom's spice cupboard, found the rosemary, rolled it up in torn pieces of white, college-ruled notebook paper, and smoked it. Why did human beings settle on tobacco leaves instead of parsley? Sage? Rosemary? Or thyme? (Somebody should write a song about this.) To my way of thinking, the advantage of smoking spices would be that you'd then die of a much more savory-smelling lung disease.

Comedian George Carlin once said that "class clowns" weren't really funnier than everybody else; they just noticed things first. They paid attention. Acutely observant.

Maybe that's a fair description of me, because the above paragraphs contain the sort of stuff I see and think about when I observe the world around me. Sometimes I think that's all I ever really do for a living — observe, listen, watch, notice. And then I talk. Or write. It explains my work as a therapist and the fruits of my life as a writer.

At a Washington, D.C., airport I had a chance encounter with a retired Episcopal priest. I spoke to him of my travails with insecure bishops and hostile church leaders. He listened, pondered, smiled a wise and knowing smile, eyes twinkling out of well-earned wrinkles, and said, "Steven, you're one of those people who point at things and give them names."

Sounds dramatic, but his little one-liner changed my life. His observation helped me take the next step of knowing myself, of firming my grasp on my own identity. His words made me neither happy nor sad; rather, clear, sober, and quiet.

The next thing he said, however, stilled my breath and chilled my bones: "I would remind you, Steven, that the Church is an institution, and institutions just aren't set up to tell the truth."

Yep. I notice stuff and then say it out loud. Sometimes folks appreciate it. Are entertained by it. Even learn from it.

Other times they hate it.

What I observe is the dance between meaning and absurdity — inextricable, inseparable, indissoluble cousins. The discovery of meaning sometimes opens like a flower. But most times it must be wrought and wrestled from absurdity. Which means we have to be willing to notice absurdity.

Life is absurd. *I'm* absurd. (So are you.) The graspings and obfuscations of the human ego are absurd. That I have any friends at all is absurd. Love is absurd. Right now as I type, all three of my children are alive and well and thriving and none of them suffer from leukemia or have bullets inside of them — it's absurd. That I'm divorced is absurd, and maybe more so that she ever loved me at all. That I'm alive or that I was ever born . . .

You have to laugh or cry. Most often these days you'll find me laughing. Irony, satire, parody, lampoon — only the truth is funny. And the truth is pretty damn funny, folks, though regularly unflattering and overwhelming.

The miracle, of course, is that out of absurdity emerges wonder and beauty and meaning. That's why I keep showing up. That's why I stay interested.

Boredom is a sin.

America is fascinated by watching people almost die

One evening in undergraduate college, my mates and I were sitting in the dormitory television lounge. It's not impossible there was beer. It certainly wasn't our fault that Arizona thought it was a good idea to let eighteen-year-olds drink in the later seventies.

We were watching a motorcycle rider doing a stunt on the show *That's Incredible*. He was trying to break his previous record-breaking performance in the Motorcycle Crash Jump. At least I think that's what it was called. None of us had ever heard of the event, let alone that someone was keeping records. It seemed this guy was gonna ride hell-bent, deliberately crashing head-on into a solid wall approximately as tall as the motorcycle's handlebars. The rider's forward momentum would then lift him off the bike and airborne. The goal of the event is to maximize the distance the rider can travel in the air.

The guy did great. Broke his own record and then some. Flew right over the mattresses that had been laid out to cushion his fall and bounced along the asphalt instead. The studio audience was delighted, and right on cue shouted out, "That's incredible!"

My friends and I were a little more subdued. Stunned, actually. My buddy broke the silence: "This show has the wrong name. It should be called "What a #@*$%." We collapsed on the floor in gales of laughter, picturing a national television studio audience calling out in unison "What a #@*$%." Did I mention there might have been beer?

Years later, I sat in a training session for suicide intervention. My teacher introduced me to the idea of "sub-intentional suicide": a death resulting from the chronically reckless behavior of someone who has no conscious desire to die.

There are some folks who can't feel alive unless they are almost dying. Some folks who consider it a point of character and heroism to constantly walk to the very edge. These people would deny they are suicidal, but the theory of sub-intentional suicide would argue that no one would consistently and deliberately risk their life and limb who did not have at least mixed feelings about their life.

And I thought of the show *That's Incredible*. And I thought of trapeze and high-wire performers who work without a net. And of those four guys on motorcycles who ride around in that round metal cage. And of auto racing. And it hit me: In America, we'll pay good money to watch you almost die. Sub-intentional suicide is an entertainment medium. Doesn't it at least seem curious?

A while back *Sports Illustrated* magazine featured a story about a couple whose vocation included setting and breaking world records for underwater descent. Once again, I had not known we were keeping such records. Yep. You go out to sea. You run a cable to the ocean floor. You take a deep breath, and a weight drags you to the appointed depth. Then you expand some balloon device that sends you racing back for the surface. The goal is to hold your breath the whole time. Or you die.

The woman died.

I tried to imagine the mother of my children explaining my death under those circumstances. Would she tell them their father was a hero? Would she say their father left them a legacy of courage and inspiration? That they could be proud and happy knowing their father died doing what he loved? Would she give them their own personal copies of the *Guinness Book of World Records* with my name in it?

Oh, she might. But I know their mother. And in her heart, I know what she'd be thinking: "What a #@*$%."

The Vietnam Memorial is one of a kind

Last weekend, Palm Mortuary brought "The Wall That Heals" to Las Vegas. It's the only authorized replica of the Vietnam Memorial.

As a growing boy with a big imagination, I remember having real anxiety about the military draft, and the idea that someday someone would place a rifle in my hands, ask me to point it at human beings across the way, and start pulling the trigger. Oh, and by the way, I would be doing this while those same human beings were pointing guns and shooting at me.

As the agony of Vietnam escalated through the late sixties and early seventies, I thought about it more and more. The law might someday require me to kill. What would it be like to be afraid for my life twenty-four hours per day? Would I die? Or, how would it change me to actually survive? How do you kill people for a couple of years, somehow avoid the countless bullets sent to kill you, and then come home and simply go to Jack in the Box? Simply mow your yard?

Hardly five weeks shy of my eighteenth birthday, President Richard Nixon pulled us out of Vietnam. Not only did I not have to enter combat as a soldier; I didn't even have to register for Selective Service. Now, at forty-eight, it seems increasingly unlikely that my government will ever ask me to kill people. Or get killed.

I'm relieved.

The Vietnam Memorial is a monument unlike any American monument. To this day I find it incredible that it was ever given serious consideration, let alone chosen, funded, constructed, and dedicated.

It's architect is a woman. An Asian woman, no less. At the time, twenty-one years old.

The Jefferson Memorial and the Lincoln Memorial are like hallowed temple grounds. The Washington Memorial is . . . well, let's just say it's decidedly masculine. The Iwo Jima Memorial is blood and guts and heroism. Most American memorials and monuments celebrate, laud, and revere. Maybe even boast.

But the Vietnam Memorial *heals*.

You walk across a commons toward the monument. But to reach the Wall, you must descend. Your footsteps are a journey downward. Within yourself.

The Wall is black — the color of mourning. As you approach the wall, you see that it is a mirror. You see yourself. This monument invites the nation to see itself.

And now the names of 58,000 dead people. You walk with maps — looking, searching. Finally your eyes locate the name of your comrade or loved one. Your arm spontaneously lifts your hand toward the wall, not even waiting for your brain's permission or direction. Your finger slowly traces the name, in one moment connecting the name, the memory, the story, the reality.

And what, exactly, is the reality? See, that's just the problem. We're not sure. Vietnam was unlike any other conflict in American history because we had no collective clarity about what it meant or who we were. The dead Americans face down in the sand at Normandy were survived by countrymen who, while broken-hearted, tended to have a clear sense of meaning in this sacrifice. Kicking Hitler's butt was necessary and costly, and this was part of the cost. But the poor guys stepping on land mines in the Vietnamese jungle? Tell me again why these people are dead?

As the Charlie Sheen character says in the opening line of the Vietnam movie *Platoon*: "Looking back, I think we were fighting ourselves."

Oh, the loss. Now the tears come. Your shoulders shake. Maybe you drop to your knees. It all pours out. The grief. The outrage. The absurdity.

To your left and right are combat medals and purple hearts and bayonets and photos and poems and letters. At other monuments, you feel humility and gratitude and pride. Here you feel humility and gratitude . . . and somehow that you want to apologize to everyone on this wall.

You ascend the steps — changed. Lighter.

Makes you wonder what we'll someday build to memorialize the soldiers fallen in the current war in Iraq.

The yin and yang of rooting for violence

On impulse, my friend buys five discounted hockey tickets. She remembers how much she liked watching hockey in college, and she invites my children and me.

I'm not a hockey fan. I haven't watched an entire hockey game since the 1980 Winter Olympics. But I tend to love excellence in most any form, and any chance at quality time with my kids is a good thing, right?

So off we go.

I like the guy who dances during the timeouts, tossing Wrangler

T-shirts to and fro. I love the energy he infuses. To boot, he's a great dancer.

I don't really get the mascot — a chartreuse, mutant biped cow named The Duke. At least I think it's a cow. But a hard-working mascot he is. And the kids love him.

And, for the record, the game couldn't have been scripted to be any more exciting. Regulation ends in a tie. Overtime ends in a tie. The shoot-out ends in a tie. The home boys win in a sudden death shoot-out. Wow. The shoot-out is my favorite part. It is so pure. Skill on skill. Speed vs. reflex. Beautiful to watch.

And that's all I want to say about hockey. Because now I'd like to talk about culture and the psychology of violence.

I must have been asleep when we agreed that 6,700 people chanting "Ref, you suck" was a perfectly fine way to behave. Oh, don't get me wrong. I can boo with the best of them, and some things deserve booing. But, "Ref, you suck" seems kinda personal and tawdry. I feel embarrassed for my children.

But about the time I work up a head of moral indignation, a hockey player from the visiting team comes out of the penalty box. "Alaska has returned to full strength," booms the PA announcer.

"But they still suck!" shout 6,700 people without missing a beat. And this time I laugh out loud. Hmm. Moral indignation erodes easily in this environment.

In the first period, play is hard and passionate. Opponents exchange baleful stares and jaw at each other. In the second period things get hotter, and the refs have to break up a handful of low-budget, push-and-shove altercations. In the third period, things really escalate. Players seem to no longer care about the location of the puck. Now checking is elbow first and aimed at the head. Helmets and gloves fly. I lose count of the fights.

And much to my surprise, the fights start to get really interesting. Yeah boy. Punch him in the head. Rock 'n' roll. Ref, you suck. Puck? What puck? I'm on my feet, heart thumping, eyes fixed on the blood and guts of five or six players and three referees, punching and thrashing and writhing. Yippee! This guys-beating-the-snot-out-of-each-other-'cause-they-can thing really grows on you!

We win. (Oh, so now it's *we*?) And the guy in front of me stands up and twirls his beer around and around. I have beer on my head. On my jacket. The lady two rows down is drenched. My children are splashed. I'm incensed. Shaking with outrage. A couple of people confront the idiot, and come to near blows. I head up the stairs for security, preferring that to having my children watch me carted off in handcuffs.

Three different ushers in maroon coats hear my tirade. Not one of them, it seems, can manage to locate security. I manage to find them myself, gathered in a little party behind a desk. And do I ever give them a piece of my mind. In turn, they take my name and phone number. Maybe they'll give me a free Wranglers hooded beer poncho.

And, of course, then it hits me. What a fool I am. I've just spent a couple of hours really enjoying watching guys on ice skates trying to dismember each other. In that same time frame, I became increasingly relaxed and even found humor in people shouting "You suck" to strangers in public. And now I'm expecting people to share my outrage about a punk with all the brains of a carp who pours beer on me and my children? Like he's done something wrong?

Like *now* I'm offended?

Addictive NASCAR fumes infiltrate racing newbie

The cloying, sweet smell of car exhaust and vaporized rubber wafts over me and 154,999 others sitting in the bright Sunday sunshine. I wonder if the brontosaurs, with their walnut-sized brains and all, every really anticipated that someday they'd become jet fuel and responsible for hurling Fiberglas boxes around in a circle at two hundred miles per hour?

I'm at my first NASCAR race. Took six days or so to drive out here, seeing as how no matter how many actual lanes of traffic are available, Las Vegans will invent three or four more. Cones, shmones.

Any card-carrying guy can mimic it with his mouth, but how do you type the Doppler Effect? VRROOoomm . . . VRROOoomm . . . VRROOoomm . . .

Pam, my dear friend and Ticket Benefactor, sits to my left; my sister and my two nephews to my right. They know the names of the actual human beings who will be driving these cars. They know that this one car is a Ford Taurus, and that this other car is a Monte Carlo. I can't see any difference between the cars except for paint job and sponsor decals.

Pam says Mark Martin (like I should know who that is) used to drive a car sponsored by Viagra. "What," I say, "they withdrew it because it got up to speed really fast and then quit?" My sister blows bubbles of laughter into her margarita. "Then it had to pull into the pit for fifteen minutes while Mark nursed a headache?"

I think you should get an award for making your little sister aspirate margarita.

I look around. What would happen to these people if, as in a sci-fi movie, they had awakened this morning to find that there were no baseball caps?

A guy beckons his buddy to take his picture, stands and removes his T-shirt. Farm boy's body. Neither fat, nor buff, nor svelte. Guy doesn't even try to flex. I guess I'm at a loss as to why his shirt is off.

Hey, that car there is sponsored by Nicorette. My ten-year-old nephew scolds me: "THAT car is Jeff Gordon's car!" Okay, so have me killed. Still, you gotta love the irony. Nicorette has decided to get out the message to stop smoking by putting its name on a machine that is going to bathe us in toxic fumes for the next three hours.

My little sister, her lungs now cleared of ice and tequila, begins to regret sitting with me.

My oldest son and I pick "our car" based on a precise, technical criterion: We decide it looks the coolest. "Who drives it?" I ask. My son shrugs: "Uh, Terry?" Fine by me. We begin to shout for Terry, which tears it for my little sister. She says she can't sit with me if I'm gonna shout "Go, Terry" every time Jeff Burton's car goes by.

My sons and I are only here to be polite. This is a concentrated slice of Americana in which I have never lived, moved, or breathed. I have never so much as paused in front of a TV screen to glance at NASCAR. But my nephews dig it. And my friend is a real sweetie. For them, it's like me going to see the Beatles.

"Gentlemen, start your engines."

My boys and I are mesmerized. Holy Toledo. Geez. Uh. Oh my. Wow. (I'm a professional writer. You shouldn't try to type like this at home.) If Jimmie Johnson came up that fast behind the car I was driving, I think I'd just wet myself and crash into the wall deliberately.

I love this. I dig these people. This subculture doesn't pretend to be anything other than what it is, which is more than I can say for the Fat Cat "being seen" in the fourth row at a Staples Center Lakers game.

Great. Just what I needed. Another expensive sports addiction.

Jeff Burton leads for a couple of laps late, but then has battery trouble. My little sister says he's "my guy" from now on, that I have to root for Jeff forever.

Fine by me. But I'll always remember him as Terry.

Dogs enrich our lives and make us more human

If the big black dog had a name, I never knew it. I see him from my driver's-side window around seven a.m. on a Saturday morning in August 1981. In the sleepy little town of Coahoma, Texas, it's not the least unusual to see a dog lying in the road, but this dog catches my eye because it thrashes helplessly in a posture nature does not permit. Something is wrong.

I investigate. There's blood mixed with the dirt. The dog's hind legs are useless. No collar. No I.D. A neighbor steps out into the front yard, and tells me the dog was struck by a car maybe an hour ago. I manage to swallow the indignation rising in my throat: *And you were just gonna watch it die in the Panhandle summer sun?*

The dog tries to lick my hand.

I walk around the corner to the sheriff's office. I tell the nice lady to please call the sheriff and have somebody send this animal to heaven right away. "Ahh wheel," she says in the bright, friendly song that pervades the natives of West Texas.

I kneel at the dog's head, and hear myself say that help is on the way. Reluctantly, I drive to work.

It's after one p.m. when I retrace my way home. The sun, unhindered by the clear blue Texas sky, bounces 104 degrees off the valiant efforts of my Toyota's air conditioner.

The dog is still there. The dog is still alive. Panting, now. Tongue caked with dirt.

My next visit to the friendly lady in the sheriff's office is less cordial than the first. Equal parts helplessness, guilt, and rage — not a pleasant cocktail. I promised mercy to The Four-Legged, and I didn't deliver. I repeat my request of earlier that morning, this time with a colorful metaphor.

In a move later nominated for Pathos of the Year, I resolve to sprint the few blocks to my home and get the dog some water. Couldn't have timed it more perfectly if I was in a stage play. Plastic jug in one hand, bowl in the other, I manage to turn the corner around the sheriff's office just in time to see the sheriff shoot the dog. Twice.

I make it back to my front stoop before I sit down and cry like the damned.

Human beings began to coax the domestic dog out of wolf and dingo DNA some 100,000 years ago. A few tribes ate them and used their fur. Other tribes used them as beasts of burden. But mostly dogs became friends, guardians, and co-workers. Their depictions guard Egyptian tombs. Native Americans saw in them totem power, and believed dogs protected them from dark forces during journeys in the spirit world. Pagans in Europe had similar ideas, but used the name 'familiars,' an idea widely misunderstood and vilified by the superstitious ignorance of Western religion.

Of course animals aren't the same as humans. When eccentric pop legend Michael Jackson says his chimpanzee is his best friend, I believe him. And I'm concerned.

But the bonds between dogs and human beings are powerful and real. Dogs are archetypal. They move us. If we'll allow it, they make us more human. They'll break our hearts.

Kelly is an Aussie shepherd mix who one day walked right off the Hopi Indian reservation into my sister's back yard. And waited for me. "Want a dog?" my sister called to ask. "Nah," I said, like I knew what the hell I was talking about.

She's here on the floor right now while I type, watching me. If I go to any other room in the house, you never have to count more than sixty seconds before she'll trot in and lie near me. I would tell you that I run two miles a day with her, but it's more like she's a sled dog pulling my sorry carcass around the neighborhood. She runs like the wind.

She's my friend. My guardian.

Which is why I can barely breathe on the evening last week when my son calls me over to say something is wrong with Kelly. Her right side is useless to her. She's in pain. No evidence of trauma. I wonder if she's poisoned. I wonder if she's had a stroke. Into the next morning, it's a mystery to the vet, too. I try to concentrate at work, but I'm waiting for the phone call that gently informs me why I'm gonna have to put her down.

The call comes. My dog, it seems, has fallen into the Golden Barrel cactus in my back yard and managed to drive cactus spines into the joints of her front and back right legs. She'll be fine.

Stupid dog.

Airport security procedures breed anxiety, humiliation

I lose a brand-new can of Edge Gel shaving cream (for sensitive skin), and a one-third-used tube of Arm & Hammer toothpaste (with added whiteners). The security lady at Bob Hope Airport, Burbank, California, shrugs, purses her lips in Classic Feminine Reproval (as if to say "Mr. Traveler, you got what was coming to you") and pitches both items into the Official Contraband Disposal Container. She lets me keep my Armani "Black Code" spray cologne and its companion deodorant stick.

So, do I, like, have a file now at the Office of Homeland Security? What, exactly, are they afraid of? "Take this plane to Cuba, or

I'll give the pilot a really close, smooth, comfortable shave"? . . .
"Surrender the cockpit, or I swear I'll vigorously brush the teeth of
everyone aboard"?

Funny thing is I had left McCarran International Airport forty-
eight hours earlier with those same menacing toiletries in plain view.
Not a peep out of our local security. Enforcement of security regulations from airport to airport around the country is only slightly
more consistent than God's eons-long struggle to make two snow-
flakes alike.

I also have a one-gallon Ziploc bag, instead of the required one-
quart size, for which I am let off with a brief lecture and warning.
I walk past a guy who's been busted with an old-fashioned baggy
and twisty-tie. The fool. He's pleading for mercy on behalf of Old
Spice Aftershave, two condoms and some tweezers. ("Get back or I
promise you that pilot will have finely groomed eyebrows *and* safe
sex before he knows what hit him!")

I watch the glamour girl behind me relinquish maybe $200 worth
of fine cosmetics. ("I'm not bluffing! Fly this plane into *It's a Small
World* at Disneyland or I'll show you what this pilot would look like
as a woman!")

The kicker has to be watching two security people leveraging a
little ol' lady up and out of her wheelchair by the armpits. A third
security person passes the wand up and down her fragile form, looking for, what . . . osteoporosis maybe. Then they ask her to take off
her shoes. You haven't seen real panic on an airplane until you've
seen a non-ambulatory granny holding Odor Eaters to the throat of
an unsuspecting airline attendant.

We're just that vulnerable.

Look, I'm not one of those ultra-liberal, American Civil Liberties
Union geektoids. I hate it when crazy, evil people take over airplanes
and crash them into buildings. I'm willing to make significant sacri-
fices to reduce the risk of that happening. To me or anyone else.

But this is nuts.

Last summer I watched, with my own eyes, a man place a carry-
on satchel on the X-ray conveyor belt, then a plastic bucket with his

jacket and shoes, then a smaller plastic dish with his keys, cell phone, and loose change . . . and then, incredibly enough, his tall plastic tumbler of ice tea. Yes. On the conveyor belt. He thought they would want to scan his beverage, I guess.

The tumbler never had a chance. They were twelve minutes cleaning it up.

On that day last summer, I remember thinking unflattering things about Iced Tea Man. Calling into question his intelligence. Specifically, I remember thinking a guy that stupid probably shouldn't be traveling alone.

But here, in the Burbank Airport, I offer Iced Tea Man a silent apology in my heart. Today, I think he wasn't stupid. He panicked. And given the sheer oddity, mounting hyper-specificity, and variable enforcement of traveling regulations, I'm ready to argue that his panic was perfectly rational.

We're like sheep. We stand in line and await our turn to be humiliated. We're unquestionably obedient to the gods of fear and unknowing.

Some days, as I slog through airport security, not sure whether to laugh maniacally or bleat, not sure if I'm watching security check or watching a sale at Payless Shoes . . . some days I give serious thought to putting *all* my clothes in the gray plastic tub and walking through the metal detector with nothing but a smile. In protest, don't you know.

If *Human Matters* is suddenly replaced by a column entitled *Meat Loaf Recipes of the World*, you'll know what happened.

American Idol turns humiliation into entertainment

1977. I'm in the student rec center at Northern Arizona University. I'm in heaven, which means I'm absorbed in a ferocious "pick-up" basketball game with the NAU varsity men's team. The NCAA won't allow official practice to begin until October 15th. So the team is just unofficially trying to kill one another until then. Gawd I love this game.

Playground pick-up basketball has an unspoken etiquette. Two teams play. A third team forms on the sidelines and declares, "We got winners." It's like putting your quarters on a pool table with a game in progress.

My team wins. A voice says, "We got winners." I look up to see a, well, a short guy. With short arms. And short legs. In tow he's got four other freshman with "really good personalities" (read: not exactly athletic). He's got to be kidding. He's been standing there watching this, right? And he still wants to play us? Why?

We execute them. 15-1. In about nine minutes. It is a minor miracle for them to successfully get the ball across half-court in any given offensive possession. How can this be fun for them? I don't get any pleasure out of humiliating people. How do they not know they don't belong at this level of competition? At once I feel pity and irritation.

I remember this as I watch (yet another) AOL film clip of Simon Cowell humiliating a contestant on *American Idol*. She weeps. He scorns.

And I don't get it.

What is she doing there? How can she not know she's, well, terrible? How can someone become a chronological adult, and be so not self-aware as to be surprised — sincerely surprised and hurt — to discover Simon not only thinks she has no talent (which she doesn't), but is personally offended by her participation in this contest.

Do friends egg these people on? I enjoy encouraging my friends to push their limits, but I'd like to think I wouldn't feed their delusions. Do the producers of *American Idol* lie bald face to a fixed percentage of talent-less singers, just so they can be sacrificed in the volcano of Mount Simon the Scornful? Just because it's great television? Or are human beings really capable of this kind of denial on their own, unmoved by data, experience, or the wincing expressions of their listeners?

A friend recently floated the theory that these people actually have very healthy egos, that we should laud these people for their courage and willingness to risk, to "shoot for the stars." I pondered the idea. Then I rejected it. Nope; there is a difference between ego strength and narcissism, between an enduring dream and a delusion.

I play guitar, but I'm no virtuoso. I can impress people who don't know anything about the guitar. I play "open mics" around town. But if Paul McCartney walked in, I wouldn't say, "Hey, Paul, listen to this." Or, "Hey, Paul's gotta sign up like everybody else and wait his turn." I would get off the stool, put my guitar in the case, and get out of Paul's way. I would consider myself lucky to be in his company.

And I think that's a function of humility. Mental health and adulthood mean accepting the things you are and are not. Real ego strength is the ability to know when it's time to contribute excellence, and when it's time to sit down and get out of the way of excellence.

I think it's great if these contestants want to sing in the shower. In the car. At the karaoke bar. With friends. Have at it. The Bible says, "Make a joyful noise to the Lord," not "Make a *pleasant* noise." Everybody should sing. It's fun. Healthy. Happy.

But if you want to compete on a national level, the expectations change. How is it some folks don't know this? I make my living in behavioral health, but I can't explain how some people can be so devoid of self-respect as to have no capacity for real self-evaluation.

A separate discussion, of course, is the skyrocketing ratings of *American Idol*. In America, humiliation is an entertainment medium. We dig it. As when we laugh at the circus clown whose pants fall down revealing polka dot underwear. Or when we thumb tabloid magazines while waiting in line at the grocery store, catching up on celebrity marriages, divorces, eating disorders, and hemorrhoid surgeries. Or when we listen to Dr. Laura talk down her nose to some stammering caller until the caller agrees he/she is a moronic, moral reprobate.

Great fun, sadism.

Taking on the devil in a world of drug addiction

I walk into hell. Hell is a one-room apartment turned crash pad for assorted cocaine addicts and dealers. The place stinks. Several days of garbage erupt knee high from the waste basket in the kitchen. The windows are covered; no one answers the phone. Paranoia rules. The sanest creature in the room appears to be the cat, ironically purring and rubbing against my leg, oblivious to the madness all around.

A family and I have come to intervene in the life of one of the living dead who abide here. We open the door, and an assortment of human beings moan and hide their eyes, crawling and rolling away from the bright sunshine pouring into the dark room. I think of late-night television vampire movies: I am Dr. Van Helsing, and we have interrupted the unnatural sleep of the captive souls who live here. They prefer to sleep through the day and rise at sunset, ready to do whatever is necessary to gorge their insatiable appetites for a new high.

But unlike the characters in Bram Stoker's novel *Dracula*, we are not armed with wooden stakes, crosses, and garlic. All we possess is the only thing that can be driven through the heart of the demon called addiction: brutal truth.

The intervention begins. I sit before this ghost, this cardboard box of what used to be a human being and take my best shot:

"This is very simple. Either you say to us, 'My name is Roxanne (not her real name) and I am a cocaine addict who wants to change,' or, you say to us, 'My life is fine . . . leave me alone.' If you say the first, we will take you to a treatment center. If you say the second, we will tell you that we love you, that we think you're going to die, and then we will leave."

She cannot put the truth into words. She says she wants to say it, but she cannot. Before our eyes is a woman wrestling with the devil, and no one can help her. It's a battle she will win or lose on her own terms. *It knows,* I think. *The demon is fighting for its life because it knows that if she tells the truth, it will die.*

She wins the battle in stages. First, she writes the truth on a scrap of paper, then she manages to read it in a faint whisper. Now she says it — out loud — and begins to weep with the relief and the pain of it. We gather her meager things and her meager self and leave.

Later that night, I am grateful to be tucked in the safety of my bed. I am exhausted — physically tired of being afraid. I have a renewed respect for the power and propensity of human beings to destroy themselves. To *want* to. Fine by me if you think I'm being dramatic, but I shall not soon forget the voice that loomed into my imagination as I opened the door. It smiled a leering smile and said, "Go ahead; try to get her out of here." And, as we departed, again: "She'll be back you know."

I don't think the voice was mine.

Bullying service workers seems to be a hobby for some

I hate to eat out with this guy, which is weird because he's a good friend, and I enjoy spending time with him in any other setting. He's smart. Affable. Well-educated. Loving husband and father. But the oddest thing happens to him in relationship to table servers. He turns into a jerk. A bully.

Do you know people like this?

From the moment the server makes first contact, my friend throws down a gauntlet. His voice becomes patiently condescending. He makes intermittent, baleful eye contact. I experience him as, well, ever so slightly paranoid. It's like my friend expects to be treated badly, and he's already gone on the offensive.

If the kitchen should be out of one of the "specials," it's a personal issue between my friend and the table server. If one of the utensils should fail my friend's inspection, he hands it to the server with the smug "Ah-HA" of a critical parent who has just busted his six-year-old trying to sneak a cookie out of the kitchen. If the server should ask for verbal clarification regarding my friend's terse murmurings, he'll pronounce the next sentence with exaggerated clarity as if he was speaking to the village idiot.

In relationship with table servers, my friend does not believe in such things as honest mistakes. Nope. All errors must be soundly and immediately punished. Heaven help the server who forgets that my friend's very dignity and personhood revolve around his preference for Thousand Island dressing "on the side."

"I asked for the dressing on the side," he says icily, shaking his head and pointing to the tragic tableau of offending greens before him.

"Of course you did . . . my mistake," the server says with all deference and humility. "I'll bring a new one right out."

"Don't bother," he says. "Just take this away."

The server is not allowed even to correct the error. There's no way back. No saving face. It's not enough to express displeasure; my friend requires that the server permanently embrace the shame of a mortal inadequacy that can never be rectified or redeemed.

Don't get me wrong: I'm fully capable of raising a ruckus if I'm treated badly. I'll ask for your manager in a heartbeat if you treat me with open disdain. I once invited a police officer to "go back to eating doughnuts." Told him that, while I appreciated his patronizing lecture about a parent's "right" to hit her daughter, I thought my mentally disturbed neighbor's dragging her daughter across the kitchen table by her hair was excessive. My bad. Don't mean to waste your time. Remember the car salesman I mentioned in last week's column? I shouted at him. His manager came out, took me for a walk, apologized on behalf of the dealership, and took $1,000 off the price of the car just like that. (Don't you hate when getting angry *works*?)

But that's not the point. Table servers, airline attendants, the teenager bagging my groceries, the guy who checks my luggage at the airport, the woman behind the paint counter at the hardware store, taxi drivers, bellhops — why do otherwise well-mannered and decent people feel entitled to treat people in service industries as peons?

Last night the Papa John's pizza guy rang my doorbell. Maybe fiftyish, I don't know. He used the three cardboard pizza boxes he was juggling as a makeshift desk and "smudged" my debit card numbers onto his receipt with a crayon. He met my eye. Good people skills. I tipped him $6. "Thank you," he said over my shoulder. He had a thick Asian accent, but I know the rush of relief and gratitude when I hear it. "People small tip tonight," he said with a bow.

As for my friend, the table server bully? Next time I eat out with this guy, I'm asking for a separate table. We'll talk by cell phone.

A cheesy boyhood dream comes true

I'm nine years old, and my father is watching the NFL title game, live from the Cotton Bowl in Dallas. Cowboys vs. Packers. The winner will play in the first Super Bowl.

"Who do you want to win?" I ask.

"The Cowboys," my dad says.

And that's all it takes for me to become a Packer fan.

The Packers won that game, and won a third consecutive title a year later against those same Cowboys in Green Bay. Then they stunk for not quite thirty years, but I hung in there. I learned to hate the Bears and the Vikings. To feel sorry for the Lions. I have a documentary about the famed Ice Bowl game on VHS.

And I nurtured a boyhood dream for these last forty years: Someday, before I die, I want my keister parked in Lambeau Field in Green Bay to watch the boys in Fort Knox gold and Kelly green. I want it to snow. I want to stand in the energy of a Lambeau tailgate party. I've always wondered what it's like to be one of those idiots who take his shirt off in minus wind chill conditions. I might or might not stoop to placing a polystyrene cheese wedge on my head. (I have my dignity.)

So, it's a little surreal to begin this column at 36,000 feet flanked by my two older sons on an AirBus bound for Green Bay. My birthday card from my wife last summer contained three tickets to: Steelers vs. Packers. Section 117. Row 4. Forty yard line. "So, go," she said.

It is *four hours* before game time and we're buried in traffic trying to exit on to Lombardi Avenue. They come from everywhere. We're told there's not a hotel room left for fifty miles in any direction.

We walk through half a mile of tailgate parties, and on to hallowed ground. Through the tunnel and into daylight. Pilgrimage complete. I cry right on cue. The only thing lacking in this moment is degrees. There are only thirty-one of them. Not nearly enough degrees, so thank God for thermal underwear.

I'm close enough to smell the grass, to hear the chatter of players warming up. Brett Favre is at midfield in a T-shirt and stocking cap. Brett is a monster sports celebrity, but in this moment he's just a guy throwing a football with friends. Okay — a guy with a catapult from the gods instead of a right arm throwing a football with friends.

I decide to interview some natives. I meet Gene, sixty-two, and his wife. Boyhood dream. Here from Mississippi. Two rows behind me is Randy, forty-two, from (*You're kidding?*) Las Vegas. Yep. Boyhood dream. It takes me several minutes to find anybody from Wisconsin, let alone from Green Bay.

But sitting right next to me is a red-haired woman who says yes, she's had these seats for a long time, and yes, she's here for most every game. How does she come to have season tickets? "My dad gave them to me," she says, and opens her coat to point to the number 77 on her Packer jersey. Oh my. I'm sitting next to Ron Kostelnik's daughter. Defensive tackle. He played in the Ice Bowl. "I was only three years old that day," she says with a shrug, "but he talked about it a lot." Ron died in 1993.

I could talk myself blue in the mouth explaining the psychodynamics of just how and why sports teams become such a powerful part of our memory, our formation, and our identity . . . how and why grown men playing a boy's game can contain for us the great dramas and archetypes of the human experience. But it would spoil it. Instead, I just decide to drink it in, to be in the moment with two precious boys, to congratulate myself for now having one less regret to ponder when I'm dying in hospice.

At the airport, I buy a polystyrene cheesehead.

So, this is my first book. Which makes it my only book. Up to now it's been a few magazine articles, a flurry of letters to the editor, my annual Christmas newsletter to family and friends, and my twice-weekly column in the *Las Vegas Review-Journal*. Now there's this book. The acknowledgments are the last leg of the journey.

It's a little overwhelming.

You see, there is nothing new under the sun. Contemplating the contributions of my teachers and mentors is like walking to the edge of a deep canyon and looking down. I can only stare into the abyss of my gratitude for so long before I have to back away breathless, shaking my head in disbelief, knowing I'll never know why and how I got so lucky to know these people who expected so much from me.

The names go on and on. Their fingerprints are all over my formation. Their life's work keeps pouring out of my mouth and flowing out of my fingertips onto this keyboard. Lou Hazlett, Deanna Scholnik, Doug Reedy, Barry Arney, Bill Nietman, Jim Biglin, Joseph Allen, Ruth Barnhouse, Leroy Howe, Rex Sprink, Bill Griffin, Jay Gray — no more, gotta back away.

Then there are the teachers I've never met. My second favorite non-human friends (right after my dog Kelly) are books. You can meet some of these friends in the bibliography. I hope there are books in heaven.

I want to thank my three sons: Jonathan, for the way he flatters me by reading my columns and sharing them with his friends; Aaron, for still speaking to me despite the frequency with which I boot him off his computer games because I'm crushed under a deadline; and Joseph, whose ritual it is to begin each morning toddling in his pajamas out of his room, into my office (he knows where to find me), and up into my lap where he curls in a ball of sublime contentment. His hair smells good. I'm never writing anything more important than that.

You've met all three of these boys in these pages. They're my teachers, too.

I want to thank Beth Lahaie, Paul Taylor, Sue Chance, Jeffery

Kirkendall, Gail Collins, and, well, my mother, Diane Kalas. What these cherished friends have in common is they are writers; their encouragement of my vocation as a writer is relentless, constant, unwavering. Isn't it cool when people who you respect believe in you?

I want to thank my editor, Geoff Schumacher. Not sure I've ever met anyone who so combines warmth, collegiality, and ease of spirit with such direct, honest communication. I feel respected. That's a big deal to me.

Carolyn Hayes Uber is the publisher of Stephens Press. It's my good fortune she believes in *Human Matters*, and I'm glad she said "yes" to this project.

I want to thank myself for *finally* daring to speak, to belly to the bar and dance naked on the table. Took me fifty years to outgrow coy and bashful and wincing and apologetic. (What was that about?)

Finally, I want to thank Sherman Frederick, publisher of the *Las Vegas Review-Journal*. *Human Matters* — the column as well as the book — exists because Sherman decided it should exist. When people ask how I landed the job of newspaper columnist, I say simply, "Because a generous friend decided to share his power to open a door of opportunity for me." It really is that simple.

If your thirst was whetted by this book, then you might find your-self wondering from what wells the water was drawn. Books are my friends, and I commend to you the following quality friendships:

The Closing of the American Mind, Allan Bloom, Simon & Schuster, 1988

Both interesting and depressing, Bloom's book convinced me that American public education no longer teaches us to think critically, nor do we as a culture particular value critical thinking. I enjoy critical thinking the way some people enjoy roller coasters.

For Your Own Good, Alice Miller, Noonday Press, 1983

Miller tracks barbarism in acculturated parenting patterns back some five hundred years, and uses the rise of Nazi Germany as a metaphor of those abusive patterns.

Couplehood, Paul Reiser, Bantam, 1995

Strange to recommend a book by a comedian/actor, but this little gem is only funny because it's true. A great book for couples to read together.

A Choice of Heroes, Mark Gerzon, Replica Books, 2003

I'd recommend this to any man, anywhere, and to any woman who has the courage to understand men better.

Mediated, Thomas De Zengotita, Bloomsbury USA, 2006

The most important — and most depressing — book I've read in twenty years. A brilliant discussion of the runaway narcissism of our culture. Made me wonder how much longer this little experiment in democracy can last. I'm not kidding.

Living Posthumously: Confronting the Loss of Vital Powers,
Andrew Bard Schmookler, Henry Holt & Co., 1997
The Denial of Death, **Ernest Becker, Free Press Paperbacks, 1998**
The Solace of Fierce Landscapes, **Belden Lane, Oxford University Press, 2007**
These three books invite the reader to consider the blessings of embracing finitude, loss, grief, and mortality. Each of them also delineates the consequences of refusing to do so.

The Enneagram, **Helen Palmer, Harper One, 1991**
Personality Types, **Don Richard Riso and Russ Hudson, Houghton Mifflin, 1996**
These two books are a terrific introduction into the Enneagram, and the wider usefulness of understanding the role of personality types in investigating what it means to be human.

The Healing Spirit: Explorations in Religion and Psychotherapy, **Paul R. Fleischman, M.D., Paragon House Publishers, 1990**
Simply the best book I've read about the overlapping frontier between religion and psychology.

He's Just Not That in to You, **Greg Behrendt and Liz Tuccillo, Simon Spotlight Entertainment, 2004**
Again, only funny because it's true. How do we so often raise women with such a precarious grasp on self?

Resurrection Sex, **David Schnarch, Harper Paperbacks, 2003**
The best book on the purpose, work, and duty of marriage ever. Schnarch uses sex as the essential metaphor of the wider dynamics of the marriage, and an accurate reflection of the personal development (and unfinished development) of the marriage participants.

Zen and the Art of Motorcycle Maintenance, **Robert Pirsig,
Bantam Books, 1975**

In my top five favorite books of all time. Hard to describe. It is at
once deeply spiritual, razor-edged academic, social and psychological. And it left me remembering one of my favorite quotes of C.G.
Jung: "The journey of individuation twice took me to the brink of
madness."

*Before Forgiving: Cautionary Views of Forgiveness in
Psychotherapy*, **Sharon Lamb and Jeffrie G. Murphy, Oxford
University Press, 2002**

This essay collection is in many ways a critique of cultural religion. The contributors want us to challenge our value of forgiveness
with the competing claims of truth and self-respect.

*The Blessing of a Skinned Knee: Using Jewish Teachings to
Raise Self-reliant Children*, **Wendy Mogel and Carrington
Macduffie, Penguin Books, 2001**

A delightful counterbalance to the runaway liberalism of modern
parenting "self-help" books.

SOURCE ARTICLES AND DATES ORIGINALLY PUBLISHED

Articles by Steven Kalas included in this book were originally published in the *Las Vegas Review-Journal*, published by Stephens Media, LLC.

We see ourselves in our children, for better or for worse   3/26/06
Adults need to remember the joy of having fun   5/13/07
Societal fears rob kids of male mentors   7/31/05
Degrading, threatening children a too-frequent pastime   6/4/06
A friend is loyal only to a friend's best interest   6/24/07
Beware the dangers of interrupting routine   7/10/05
A Father's Day challenge: Be a better role model   6/18/06
Father-son bond strengthened through gun education   12/31/06
Corporal punishment does more harm than good   5/20/07
We usually know when it's time to go home   8/27/06
Superhero myths reveal man's struggle with power, intimacy
  4/9/06
Men, women have built-in communication preferences   12/12/06
Why do women always fall for the bad boys?   9/10/06
Neither gentleman nor jerk is the right approach   2/25/07
Sexual harassment is more complicated than just sex   4/30/06
Masculinity defies a simple definition   4/15/07
Sexual courtship is an uneven two-way street   10/9/05
Clichés, curiosities abound in online dating world   9/24/06
What's on the outside matters, too   3/27/05
Reconsider the true meaning of narcissism   11/19/06
Anger and violence are disguises for grief and loss   9/25/05
Vitality and self-respect are sexually attractive   5 weeks in 2006
To understand ambiguity takes clarity of vision   2/27/05
There's no reason to apologize for tears   10/8/06
Grieving parents need to show kids optimistic side   2/4/07
Amish teach valuable lessons about fear   10/15/06
Common responses to pain of loss are not useful   9/17/06
Finding the right words to say to sad people   10/10/06

About the Author

Born and raised in Phoenix, Arizona, Steven Kalas earned a bachelor's degree in psychology from Northern Arizona University and a master's in theology from Southern Methodist University. He works as an individual, marriage, and family counselor and pastoral counselor in Las Vegas, Nevada. Steven's column, *Human Matters*, is published Sundays and Tuesdays in the *Las Vegas Review-Journal*. Steven is a former Episcopal priest turned counselor and freelance writer. He does stand-up comedy, and travels nationally as a public speaker. He writes songs and performs in the band PaperCymbal (www.stevenkalas.com). Steven has three sons: Jonathan, 16, Aaron, 14, and (what was he thinking?) Joseph, age 5. He is a rabid Phoenix Suns fan, a crazed Green Bay Packers fan, a Beatlemaniac, and owns DVD recordings of every known work of Monty Python's Flying Circus.

Other Stephens Press Books of Interest

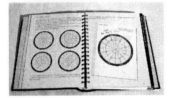

You Are More Than Enough and the
You Are More Than Enough Achievement Journal
You Are More Than Enough is a powerful guide to discovering your purpose, unleashing your passion, and shaping your habits to realize the success you want in all the areas of your life — personal and professional relationships, career, finances, and security. The moment you start to apply what you read in this book, you'll come to the realization that you really are . . . **more than enough.** The daily *Achievement Journal* helps you track your progress toward achieving your goals and become a better YOU. Author: Judi Moreo

Text: ISBN-13: 978-1932173-727 ....$24.95 Hardcover.
Journal: ISBN-13: 978-1932173-659..................$19.95 Hardcover.

Dancing in my Nightgown
When Betty loses her husband Denny to cancer after almost 49 years of marriage, widowhood forces Betty to find out what she can do on her own. She has a lot to learn, having never been single before. These short, upbeat, inspiring stories tell us how this spunky septuagenarian survives—she decides to dance instead of sitting on the sidelines. Betty laughs and cries her way through grief and, ultimately, comes to see her situation as normal. "None of us is going to get out of this alive, and someone is always going to be left behind feeling sad." Author: Betty Auchard
ISBN-13: 978-1932173-758..$16.95 Trade Paper.

Order Books: StephensPress.com Or Call 888-951-BOOK

STEPHENS PRESS, LLC
A Stephens Media Company

1111 W. Bonanza Road • Las Vegas, Nevada 89106